SOCIAL WORK LAW

Applying the Law in Practice

Other books you may be interested in

Dilemmas and Decision Making in Social Work
Abbi Jackson   9781914171208

Social Work and Covid-19: Lessons for Education and Practice
Edited by Denise Turner   9781913453619

Out of the Shadows: The Role of Social Workers in Disasters
Edited by Angie Bartoli, Maris Stratulis and Rebekah Pierre   9781915080073

*The Anti-racist Social Worker: Stories of Activism by Social Care and
Allied Health Professionals*
Edited by Tanya Moore and Glory Simango   9781914171413

Our titles are also available in a range of electronic formats. To order, or for details of our bulk discounts, please go to our website www.criticalpublishing.com or contact our distributor Ingram Publisher Services, telephone 01752 202301 or email NBNi.Cservs@ingramcontent.com

CRITICAL
PUBLISHING

SOCIAL WORK LAW

Applying the Law in Practice

Michelle Evans and Denise Harvey

First published in 2022 by Critical Publishing Ltd

British Library Cataloguing in Publication Data
A CIP record for this book is available from the British Library

ISBN: 9781914171802

This book is also available in the following e-book formats:
EPUB ISBN: 9781914171819
Adobe e-book ISBN: 9781914171826

Cover and text design by Out of House Ltd
Project management by Newgen Publishing UK

Critical Publishing
3 Connaught Road
St Albans
AL3 5RX

www.criticalpublishing.com

Printed on FSC accredited paper

Contents

Endorsement

This highly readable book is a great guide for students seeking to understand the range of relevant legislation. The use of case studies really brings the law to life, making it easier to understand and remember. The materials are attractive and colour-coded, which enables students to link the law more clearly. The study skills chapter designed to help students with law essays and law exams is particularly innovative and helpful. An authoritative but accessible guide that should be required reading.

Dr Andrew Whittaker, Professor of Social Work
Research, London South Bank University

Meet the authors

Dr Michelle Evans

Michelle is a published author, filmmaker, placement link lecturer, Senior Fellow of the Higher Education Academy and senior lecturer at London South Bank University (LSBU), where she is module lead teaching law for social workers at master's level. Michelle takes great pride in finding innovative and interesting ways to engage and teach students to enable them not only to reach their full potential in terms of assignment grades but to take academic learning and apply it in social work practice, increasing students' personal professional development.

Denise Harvey

Denise is a qualified social worker with over 21 years' experience working within various areas of children and families' services. She is a Fellow of the Higher Education Academy (FHEA) and professional lead for social work at LSBU. Having significant current practice experience in both the youth court and the family court, she uses her practice skills as the module lead on the undergraduate 'Law for Social Work' module. Denise is an experienced and published researcher, whose areas of expertise include youth justice law, risk and decision making. She is currently undertaking her PhD.

1   Introduction to using this book

INTRODUCTION

This book is designed to enable you to understand, apply and use the law in your social work practice. The idea for the book emerged as a result of an online survey to ascertain the learning needs of social work students studying law. In addition, we also consulted with students to identify their learning needs and what they would like to be taught when undergoing academic and practical social work law studies. Sometimes social work students, newly qualified practitioners or practitioners who are embarking on a new area of practice are unsure of the intricacies of the law and how to apply it in practice or they may find it daunting and intimidating. This book has been designed not only to support you, as a social work student, in your academic studies and on placement, but also to help newly qualified social workers, developing practitioners, practice educators, on-site supervisors and lecturers to understand and apply the law effectively.

Each chapter is written as we teach, by using a variety of techniques to make law more accessible, understandable and less daunting; for example, mindmaps, case studies, a discussion around how the decisions were made on the case studies, key points to remember and tasks to test your legislative knowledge (answers are at the back of the book). Throughout you are encouraged to conduct research yourself, as wider reading increases knowledge and contributes to presenting arguments in a more succinct and analytical way.

At the end of each chapter there is also the opportunity to consider if any anti-discriminatory practices or any anti-oppressive practice issues stood out for you, as well as activities to capture personal reflection and individual thoughts.

Reflection can be described as critically evaluating and analysing situations and experiences, thinking about what you have done, how you did it, what went well and what could have been done better (Brown and Rutter, 2008; Rutter and Brown, 2019) and therefore is beneficial for effective social work practice. Professor Donald Schön (1983, 1987) conceptualised two types of reflection in practice: reflection on action, for example thinking about something you have already done, and reflection in action, for example thinking about what you are doing at the time you are doing it (Brown and Rutter, 2008). At the end of each chapter, you are encouraged to reflect on what you have learned and record your own personal feelings, perhaps writing it in your own personal copy of this book, so that you have a quick reference should you wish to refer to it in the future. A variety of reflective models are considered in the chapters: for example, Chapter 6 considers Kolb's (1984) reflective cycle, Chapter 7 examines the weather model of reflection (Maclean, 2016), while Chapter 10 explores Gibbs' (1988) reflective cycle.

In our lectures we use colour coding to present material to enable students to easily identify areas of legislation; therefore, chapter headings have been colour coded to facilitate cross-referencing with the mindmaps. For example, the child legislation chapter headings in Chapters 3, 4 and 5 are in pink; Chapter 6 on the Mental Capacity Act 2005 is in yellow; Chapter 8 on the Mental Health Act 1983/2007 is in red; while Chapter 10 on the Care Act 2014 is in green.

To give you an idea of the topics that are covered in this book, each chapter is briefly introduced here. The next chapter, Chapter 2, considers the English legal system, with Chapters 3, 4 and 5 focusing on various aspects of child legislation such as child in need (s17) or risk of significant harm (s47), when children become looked after (s20, s31, s38) and children in the criminal justice system. Chapter 6 looks at the Mental Capacity Act 2005 with Chapter 7 exploring Deprivation of Liberty Safeguards (DoLS), Liberty Protection Safeguards (LPS) and the Mental Capacity (Amendment) Act 2019. The next two chapters, Chapters 8 and 9, reflect upon legislation that can affect both children and adults, with Chapter 8 primarily focusing on the Mental Health Act 1983 and the 2007 amendment and Chapter 9 considering various legislation pertaining to impairment seen and unseen. Next, Chapter 10 turns its attention to adult care and support and discusses who would be eligible (s13) by concentrating on the Care Act 2014. Chapter 11 is something a little bit different for a law textbook as it focuses on study skills, providing you with some skills and techniques for not only applying the law in practice but how you could approach your exam or essay on your social work course and when training in placement. You will also see the sections of the law referred to, as has been done above, so for example when referring to an assessment under the Care Act 2014, section 9 would be referred to; this is to help you to see how easy it is to apply sections of the law when working with vulnerable adults and children in your social work practice to support and safeguard.

WHY IS IT IMPORTANT TO UNDERSTAND HOW TO USE THE LAW IN PRACTICE?

Although you are not expected to become a legal expert, as a social worker student, it is essential that you reflect upon the fact that social work is a people profession where social workers manage risk and use the law only when needed and in a person-appropriate way. This is important because, as you will learn as you journey through the case studies, in every decision you make you will need the law to guide you.

THE DIFFERENCE BETWEEN GUIDANCE AND ACTS OF PARLIAMENT

There is a difference between guidance and Acts of Parliament. Guidance is just what it says, guidance, it is not compulsory. However, if guidance is not adhered to and something goes wrong you can be liable to judicial review. So, for example, guidance such as *Working Together to Safeguard Children* (HM Government, 2018) or *What to Do If You Are Worried a Child Is Being Abused* (HM Government, 2015) could be used to improve practice or give guidance if a serious issue arises. Let's consider the guidance *Working Together to Safeguard Children* (HM Government, 2018); this document provides guidance on the actions required by professionals when a child dies suddenly, for example: inform agency, the need for a rapid response, how to provide support to the family, how to refer to specialist support services and also how to seek support for yourself, your own mental health and well-being (supervision/counselling services). Thus, although documents such as these are guidance, you can see how they benefit not just social work professionals but all professionals who work to safeguard and support vulnerable people.

An Act of Parliament creates a new law or changes an existing law. An Act is a bill that has been approved by both the House of Commons and the House of Lords and been given Royal Assent by the Monarch. Acts of Parliament are compulsory and it is an offence not to uphold the law; examples of Acts of Parliament are the Children Act 1989 and the 2004 amendment, the Mental Capacity Act 2005 and the 2009/2019 amendments, the Care Act 2014, and the Mental Health Act 1983 and the 2007 amendment (for more information, see UK Parliament, 2022).

REFERENCES

Brown, K and Rutter, L (2008) *Critical Thinking for Social Work*. London: Learning Matters Ltd/Sage.

Gibbs, G (1988) *Learning by Doing: A Guide to Teaching and Learning Methods*. Oxford: Further Education Unit, Oxford Polytechnic.

HM Government (2015) *What to Do If You Are Worried a Child Is Being Abused*. [online] Available at: https://assets.publishing.service.gov.uk/government/uploads/system/uploads/attachment_data/file/419604/What_to_do_if_you_re_worried_a_child_is_being_abused.pdf (accessed 7 March 2022).

HM Government (2018) *Working Together to Safeguard Children*. [online] Available at: https://assets.publishing.service.gov.uk/government/uploads/system/uploads/attachment_data/file/942454/Working_together_to_safeguard_children_inter_agency_guidance.pdf (accessed 7 March 2022).

Maclean, S (2016) A New Model for Social Work Reflection: Whatever the Weather. *Professional Social Work*, March: 28–9.

Rutter, L and Brown, K (2019) *Critical Thinking and Professional Judgement for Social Work*. London: Sage.

Schön, D (1983) *The Reflective Practitioner: How Professionals Think in Action*. London: Temple Smith.

Schön, D (1987) *Educating the Reflective Practitioner*. San Francisco: Jossey-Bass.

UK Parliament (2022) What is an Act of Parliament? [online] Available at: www.parliament.uk/about/how/laws/acts (accessed 4 March 2022).

2   The English legal system in relation to social work practice

INTRODUCTION

This chapter starts with a disclaimer: *my aim is not to make you a legal professional* but rather to consider the law as it relates specifically to social work practice within the wider context of the English legal system. This is something I find myself saying to students at the beginning of the semester when teaching the law module as part of the social work programme. Often students believe that taking the social work law module is like doing a law degree in 12 weeks, when in fact it is about gaining knowledge of the law and how it applies directly to the work we do as social workers. Have you ever considered how people who are not trained in law come to know about it? Well, it is simple; it is by practice and legal advice from trained family lawyers whose job it is to practise law.

Having a degree in law is not a prerequisite to becoming a social worker

The Professional Capabilities Framework (PCF 5–Knowledge) outlines clearly that at the prequalifying entrance point students (including Assessed and Supported Year in Employment) should:

> *Develop and apply relevant knowledge from social work practice and research, social sciences, law, other professional and relevant fields, and from the experience of people who use services. We develop our professional knowledge throughout our careers and sustain our curiosity. As a unified profession, we develop core knowledge that relates to our purpose, values, and ethics. We also develop specific knowledge needed for fields of practice and roles. Our knowledge comes from social work practice, theory, law, research, expertise by experience, and from other relevant fields and disciplines. All social workers contribute to creating as well as using professional knowledge. We understand our distinctive knowledge complements that of other disciplines to provide effective services.*
>
> (British Association of Social Workers, 2018)

WHAT IS THE LAW?

Let us begin by understanding what the law is. Laws are essentially a complex system of customs, traditions, regulations and rules which state how we must behave. There are three main components that make laws different from simple societal rules.

1. Laws are set and established and enforced by government.

2. Laws are compulsory.

3. Laws involve consequences, which are enforced through the legal system (in the UK this is usually the courts though it can also be tribunals).

    The law can also be defined as a system of rules and regulations to govern society, things made by judges, means by which people can seek justice and/or reparation, rules which keep society manageable, rules which serve to oppress and or control society.

    (Partington, 2021)

Rules on the other hand denote something about morally accepted behaviours that help people to understand how they should behave (Partington, 2021).

Law-making system in England and Wales

We often hear about laws being made in the Houses of Parliament; this is the main law-making body. The link between Parliament and the Court is that any legislation passed by Parliament is then accepted by the Court and understood that this take pre-eminence over any common law (law that is made by the judge through cases).

Head of state

The relationship between Parliament and the state is that most laws are exercised by the government in the name of the monarch. The Queen (Elizabeth II) is the current monarch and the head of state. Her primary role as the monarch is to remain legally responsible for any powers that the government exercises in law.

Structure

The UK Parliament comprises two separate Houses: the House of Commons and the House of Lords.

The House of Commons is a representative body, the membership of which is elected, and it has legislative powers (ie laws that the Commons has the sovereignty to make). The leader of the party in power (the prime minister) chooses their cabinet, which is made up of members from that political party who are also members of the House of Commons (MPs).

The House of Lords is not elected and is not a representative body. Most members of the House of Lords are life peers appointed under the Life Peerages Act 1958. Such peers are appointed by the monarch on the advice of the prime minister, who receives advice on who to put forward from a non-political Appointments Commission (Rabb, 2021).

THE LAW WITHIN THE ENGLISH LEGAL SYSTEM

The law is embedded within the English legal system, which is constituted of:

○   law-making bodies, eg parliament, judiciary, legislature;

○   those that enforce the law;

○   institutions, processes and personnel that contribute to the operation and enforcement of the law;

○   workings of the courts and tribunals;

○   legal professionals;

○   police, prosecutors and jurors;

○   organisations that support access to justice, eg Citizen Advice Bureau, legal aid, law shops, advocacy projects.

Sources of law in the English legal system

The sources of law cover the principles that include legislation, common law, statutes, bills and delegated legislation.

Legislation

Legislation is the law created by the legislature (people elected to make law for a state). It mainly deals with Acts of Parliament. The UK Parliament is the body that has the power to pass laws that can be applied in all four countries. The UK Parliament consists of the House of Lords and House of Commons.

Common law

Common law is derived from the judicial decisions of courts and similar tribunals. The English legal system of England and Wales is a common law one.

Statutes

Statutes are formally written down law which has been executed by a legislative body other than Parliament – Parliaments pass Acts.

Bill

A bill is a proposed law which has been discussed and debated in Parliament. It is then approved by Parliament and goes on to receive royal assent and becomes law.

Delegated legislation

Delegated legislation is an Act of Parliament that may give a minister or some other party the rights to make legal provisions.

LEGAL JURISDICTION

Legal jurisdiction is defined as the extent of power to make legal decisions and judgements within a defined geographical area. The courts in England and Wales have legal jurisdiction to try cases in relation to offences committed in the UK and a single legal system known as the English legal system. Ireland and Scotland have their own legislation, as do other areas that are not strictly part of the UK, such as the Isle of Man and the Channel Islands (which are Crown dependencies). Wales is currently looking at its own jurisdiction having law-making legislature, but no jurisdiction presents as incongruent for Wales.

In England you only need to concern yourselves with English and European laws unless you go on to practise in other parts of the UK (EU legislation applied until 31 December 2020). England and Wales currently have the same laws though Wales is developing its own legal system. Scotland and Ireland have completely different legal systems (Scottish Law Online, 2021).

THE COURTS IN ENGLAND AND WALES

If like me, you are a visual learner, describing the structure of the English Legal system would be lost on you. Figure 2.1 offers a pictorial representation of the structure of the English legal system and its different branches.

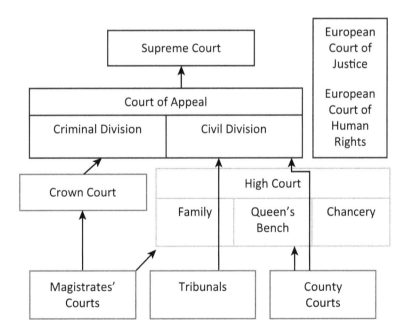

Figure 2.1 The English legal system structure

The courts in England play an important role in the execution of the law in relation to different parts of the law. There are different courts that deal with different matters; those that relate specifically to social work practice are highlighted below.

Magistrates' Courts

These courts hear all criminal cases at first instance. Less serious cases and those involving juveniles are tried in the Magistrates' Courts, as well as some civil cases. Magistrates deal with three kinds of offence: summary (less serious cases), either way (cases that can be heard either in a Magistrates' Court or before a judge and a jury in the Crown Court) and indictable only (serious cases).

The Family Court

The Family Court was established in 2014 and sits within the Magistrates' Court. It has national jurisdiction and brings all levels of family judiciary to sit together in the same court.

The County Court

There are approximately 160 county courts that hear cases within their geographic catchment area. These courts deal with civil (non-criminal and non-family) cases. The County Court hears (subject to exceptions) money claims with a value up to and including £100,000 and claims for damages for personal injury with a value up to £50,000. Cases are ordinarily held where the defendant resides.

The Crown Court

The Crown Court sits in centres around England and Wales. This court deals with indictable (meaning it can be tried by jury) criminal cases that are transferred from the Magistrates' Courts, including serious criminal cases. The Old Bailey is a type of Crown Court.

The High Court

The High Court has jurisdiction for more serious and complex civil and family cases at first instance. It contains three divisions: Queen's Bench, Family and Chancery. The Queen's Bench Division is the biggest of the three High Court Divisions. Included within it are a number of specialist courts: the Admiralty, Commercial, Mercantile, Technology and Construction, and Administrative Courts. The Chancery Division deals with company law, partnership claims, conveyancing, land law, probate, patent and taxation cases. This division has three specialist courts: the Companies Court, the Patents Court and the Bankruptcy Court. The area that relates to social work is the Family Division, which deals with cases that pertain to children and appeals from family proceedings, cases which have been transferred from one of the lower courts (such as County Court or Family Court).

The Court of Appeal

The Court of Appeal and the High Court constitute the 'senior courts' of England and Wales. The Court of Appeal is an appellate court and is divided into two divisions,

Criminal and Civil. It is useful to understand this particular court as often in cases where parents appeal a decision made by the local authority, it will be heard at this court.

The Supreme Court

The Supreme Court is the final court of appeal in the UK. It hears appeals on arguable points of law of public importance for the whole of the UK in civil cases, and for England and Wales and Northern Ireland in criminal cases. In Scotland, appeals can be made from the lower courts in criminal cases to the High Court of Justiciary. The Judicial Committee of the Privy Council, which comprises justices of the Supreme Court and some senior Commonwealth judges, is the final court of appeal for a number of Commonwealth countries, as well as the UK's overseas territories, Crown Dependencies and military sovereign bases (Supreme Court Online, 2021).

DIFFERENT COURTS THAT RELATE TO SOCIAL WORK PRACTICE

Having identified the different courts within the English legal system, in this section we will take a closer look at the ones that most closely relate to social work practice. In children social work practice, we are concerned with the functioning and use of the Family Court; with adults we are concerned with the Court of Protection, tribunals, Magistrate, and Crown Courts (in criminal proceedings); while within youth justice we are concerned with the Magistrates' Court which becomes a Youth Court and the Crown Court.

Family Court

The Family Court deals with the following in relation to children and young people:

○ parental disputes over the upbringing of children;

○ local authority intervention to protect children;

○ decrees relating to divorce;

○ financial support for children after divorce or relationship breakdown;

○ some aspects of domestic violence;

○ adoption.

Court of Protection

We will examine the Court of Protection in more detail in Chapter 6 on mental capacity.

Youth Court

The Youth Court is a criminal court that deals with young people who offend. A traditional Magistrates' Court then sits as a Youth Court. For more detail, see Chapter 5 on youth justice.

The main criminal courts in England in Wales are:

○   the Magistrates' Courts;

○   the Youth Court – for ages 10–17 (part of the Magistrates' Court);

○   the Crown Court.

All criminal offences are classified as one of the following:

○   summary only offences, which are offences that are only tried at a Magistrates' Court and cannot be tried by a jury, eg public order offences or minor criminal damage;

○   either way offences, triable in either the Magistrates Court or the Crown Court, eg theft or deception;

○   indictable only offences, triable only in the Crown Court and serious enough offences that warrant a trial by jury, eg sex offences, grievous bodily harm or murder.

TYPES OF LAW THAT RELATE TO SOCIAL WORK PRACTICE

As social work is a profession that deals with people as well as the state, this will invoke a different part of the law to come into effect. Phrases like public law and private law are common occurrences in social work language.

Public law

Public law deals with areas in which society, the government or the state has decided to interfere in a direct manner with the behaviour of individuals, for example care proceedings where the state has set parameters in the relevant legislation (Children Act 1989) for how children should be brought up. In extreme circumstances, the state in the form of the local authority will step in and take over the upbringing of children by accessing orders through the court that allow them to take on parental responsibilities. Many arguments for the interference of the state in family life surround the human rights of that individual (Article 8 of the Human Rights Act 1998, right to private and family life) and how much of a restriction or oppression the state poses if it interferes with it. The key in social work practice is about the balance of state control through the application of the law and safeguarding duties in legislation, and people's human right to freedom and to live their lives.

Public law cases brought by local authorities or an authorised person (currently only the NSPCC) include matters such as:

○   care orders, which give parental responsibility for the child concerned to the local authority applying for the order;

○   supervision orders, which place the child under the supervision of their local authority;

○   emergency protection orders, which are used to ensure the immediate safety of a child by taking them to a place of safety, or by preventing their removal from a place of safety.

Public law cases must start in the Family Proceedings Courts. They may be transferred to the County Courts if it will minimise delay or enable the case to be merged with other family proceedings, or where the matter is unusually grave, complicated or important (Judiciary UK, 2021).

Private law

Private law deals with mediating the behaviour of individuals, for example a dispute between a customer and shop over the quality of a purchase or a dispute between parents who have decided to separate or divorce.

Private law cases are brought by private individuals, generally in connection with divorce or the parents' separation.

Order types include:

o   parental responsibility;

o   financial applications;

o   special guardianship orders, which give a special guardian legal responsibility without removing legal responsibility from the birth parents.

Section 8: Private law orders

Any parent, guardian or special guardian, step-parent with parental responsibility for the child, or person with a child arrangement order can apply for any section 8 order. There are four types of section 8 orders available.

o   Child arrangement order: these determine who a child lives with.

o   Contact order: these require the person with whom the child lives to allow the child to have contact with a named person; the order may set out the arrangements for contact. Child arrangement and contact orders can also be applied for by a person with whom the child has lived for at least three years, or any party to a marriage or civil partnership (whether or not subsisting) where the child is a child of the family.

o   Prohibited steps order: these are used to prevent an action which could be exercised by someone with parental responsibility from being taken without the consent of the court; for example, a prohibited steps order is made restraining the removal of the child from the county or from their home to prevent relocation.

o   Specific issues order: these are usually used to resolve areas of disagreement relating to the exercising of parental responsibility.

These will be covered in more depth in Chapter 3 of the book.

Importantly, and perhaps an unnecessary added complication as is the case with the law, is that there is always an exception to the rule, which we shall call the cross-over, where two laws meet.

Cross-over

In the case of divorce proceedings (which is private law as it is a dispute between two individuals), if there is concern about a child's welfare, there are powers for the local authority to investigate within the provisions of the Children Act 1989 (public law).

The overlap: an example

Mikel is nine years old and following the suicide of his father his mother became clinically depressed and was unable to care for him. She developed a serious problem with cannabis. Social workers found him poorly clothed, hungry, severely neglected and living in rented accommodation with no furniture or heating. His mother had sold all of the property in the accommodation and was working as a prostitute from the address. Mikel was removed from the home under the Children Act 1989 (s44) by means of an emergency protection order (EPO), which was applied for through the Family Court, and placed with foster carers (the welfare of the child, the Children Act 1989, s1, and the need to protect him is public law). Investigations revealed a large and supportive family in Wales and maternal grandparents who were willing to care for him. They would need to apply for a child arrangement order (CAO, private law section 8 orders under the Children Act 1989) to allow him to live with them and give them parental responsibility. This process would be managed through the Family Court.

Civil versus criminal law

Civil law is a form of private law and involves the relationships between individual citizens where there is a dispute that highlights that individual's or organisation's rights and property. It is the legal mechanism through which individuals can bring claims against others and have those rights decided and enforced. The purpose of civil law is to resolve disputes between individuals and to provide solutions; it is not concerned with punishment as such. Civil cases are identified by reference to the names of the parties involved in the dispute, for example, *Johnson v Johnson* (Slapper and Kelly, 2009). Criminal law relates to crime and offending and any breaches that will have an impact on society as a whole. This area of the law pertains to what Acts of Parliament are deemed to be acceptable (and unacceptable) conduct in the UK.

Case study

Let us refer back to Mikel's case study. We will consider which parts of the law relate to him, which court the cases will be heard in and what our role will be in the case.

Mikel is nine years old and following the suicide of his father his mother became clinically depressed and was unable to care for him. She developed a serious problem with cannabis. Social workers found him poorly clothed, hungry, severely neglected and living in rented accommodation with no furniture or heating. His mother had sold all of the property in the accommodation and was working as a prostitute from the address. Investigations revealed a large and supportive family in Wales and maternal grandparents who were willing to care for him.

THE SOCIAL WORK ROLE

When looking at legislation, social workers need to see whether there is a 'duty' or 'power' to act. It is important to get an understanding of the distinction between the two.

- If there is a **duty** placed on a local authority or social worker then, whatever that duty is, it has to be carried out.

- If a local authority or social worker is provided with the **power** to undertake an act, then there is no obligation to carry out that act.

Consider the following example.

- Duty: s20 of the Care Act 2014 says a local authority '***must** meet the adult's needs for care and support which meet the eligibility criteria*'.

- Power: para 16 of Sch.2, Children Act 1989, says '*The authority **may** make payments to a parent of a child in respect of travelling*'.

Where there is a duty, we must act, and where there is a power, it is down to discretion.

Decisions made on the case

My initial thoughts on this case are that this could be one of private law and heard in the family court. This deals with a matter between individuals and is potentially about who can look after Mikel (remember the section 8 orders).

However, as the case study progresses, we now see the need for the state to become involved under section 1 of the Children Act 1989 as there are concerns over Mikel's welfare and his mother's parenting capacity (as defined in the framework for assessing children in need). As noted in the case study, Mikel's mother is clinically depressed and unable to care for him; she developed a serious problem with cannabis. The state's intervention is via a local authority social worker who has a duty to intervene when they have concerns about the welfare of a child (Mikel was found poorly clothed, hungry, severely neglected and living in rented accommodation with no furniture or heating. His mother had sold all of the property in the accommodation and was working as a prostitute from the address). The issue now becomes one of where Mikel can reside and who can take on the responsibility for his care. Mikel was removed from the home under the Children Act 1989 (s44) by means of an emergency protection order (EPO), which was applied for through the family court by the social worker, and placed with foster carers (the welfare of the child, Children Act 1989, s1). The need to protect him is public law because this is a matter between the individual and the state.

While placing Mikel in foster care is a good short-term plan, with family members available to help and support, the local authority needs to exercise its powers to plan for the long-term care of Mikel. Mikel's family in Wales would need to apply for a child arrangement order to allow him to live with them and give them parental responsibility. This process would be managed through the Family Court as all applications can be made through the court.

WHEN THE LAW MIGHT BE APPLIED IN HEALTH AND SOCIAL CARE

While the case study above gives an example of when the law might be applied, there are a number of different scenarios listed below which also represent conditions in which the law can or might be applied in all areas of health and social care; it is not an exhaustive list, but seeks to illustrate just how vast the law is:

o   criminal law, eg when a crime is committed;

o   civil law, eg negligence – when there is a dispute between individuals;

o   professional liability;

o   employment law;

o   health and safety;

o   professional registration and accountability;

o   confidentiality and access to medical records;

o   statements, records and giving evidence;

o   capacity and competence;

o   consent;

o   benefits and social housing;

o   data protection;

o   DoLS (Deprivation of Liberty Safeguards);

o   safeguarding;

o   family law;

o   drugs;

o   property;

o   birth, abortion, reproductive rights;

o   end of life care and death;

○   last rites and disposal of the body;

○   mental health law;

○   handling complaints;

○   consent and information giving;

○   ensuring patients'/clients' rights;

○   'whistleblowing'/duty of candour.

Professionals in the court services

Part of a social worker's role is to attend court and present reports, specialist assessment and to be expert witnesses. Attending court can be quite daunting and challenging, but below is a list of different professionals who are part of the court services and who you can expect to see if you attend court:

○   barristers (prosecution and defence);

○   solicitors and legal executives;

○   magistrates;

○   court clerk;

○   ushers;

○   jurors;

○   judges (different levels);

○   police officers;

○   social workers – *you*;

○   probation and youth offending officers;

○   guardians;

○   expert witnesses – this could also be *you*;

○   security and prison officers.

Key points to remember

This chapter has given you a good flavour of the English legal system in a manner that is student friendly and has allowed you to engage with the information positively. Remember that social work as a profession does not require you to be legally trained. The PCFs talk about knowledge of the law, so the process you

→

should engage in is becoming familiar with the aspects of the law that deal directly with your practice. Make a list of the different types of social work practice that we engage in and then list alongside it the legislation that relates to it.

○ The English legal system is made up of legislation that relates to England and Wales, with specific jurisdiction for any matters of law in the named geographical area. The different courts that exist have specific roles and powers within legislation.

TEST YOUR LEGISLATIVE KNOWLEDGE

Answers are at the back of the book.

Questions

● Name five people you can expect to see if you attend court.

● What are the three main characteristics that make laws different from simple rules?

● What seven things constitute the English legal system?

● What are the three main criminal courts in England and Wales?

- Name three courts a social worker might attend.

- What is the difference between a duty and a power?

- Name one difference between private law and public law.

- Name at least four types of courts and explain what they do.

CHAPTER SUMMARY

The English legal system is the main context for law relating to social care. Within this complex system there are courts and practices that relate to social work practice. This chapter has looked at the different spheres within the legal system, the courts, and their defined roles as well as social work practice within these systems. Courts such as the Family Court, Crown Court and Court of Appeal deal with matters relating to social work practice. Legislation places a duty and gives powers to the local authority to intervene.

END OF CHAPTER ACTIVITY TO CAPTURE PERSONAL REFLECTIONS AND INDIVIDUAL THOUGHTS

Critically reflect on this chapter and what you have learned, recording your own personal thoughts and feelings. The reflective model you might like to consider in this chapter is Gibbs' (1988) model of reflection. Also consider if there are any anti-discriminatory or any anti-oppressive practice issues (Equality Act 2010) that stand out for you.

Capture your personal reflections and individual thoughts here

REFERENCES

British Association of Social Workers (2018) Professional Capabilities Framework. [online] Available at: www.basw.co.uk/professional-development/professional-capabilities-framework-pcf/the-pcf/social-worker/knowledge (accessed 29 November 2021).

Children Act 1989 [online] Available at: www.legislation.gov.uk/ukpga/1989/41/contents (accessed 4 March 2022).

Care Act 2014 [online] available at: www.legislation.gov.uk/ukpga/2014/23/contents (accessed 4 March 2022).

Equality Act 2010 [online] Available at: www.legislation.gov.uk/ukpga/2010/15/contents (accessed 4 March 2022).

Gibbs, G (1988) *Learning by Doing: A Guide to Teaching and Learning Methods*. Further Education Unit. Oxford: Oxford Polytechnic.

Health and Social Care Act 2012, *c.7*. [online] Available at: www.legislation.gov.uk/ukpga/2012/7/contents/enacted (accessed 4 March 2022).

Judiciary UK (2021) Courts and Tribunal Judiciary. [online] Available at: www.judiciary.uk (accessed 27 November 2021).

Partington, M (2021) *Introduction to the English Legal System*. Oxford: Oxford University Press.

Rabb, S (2021) Serle Court. [online] Available at: www.serlecourt.co.uk (accessed 4 March 2022).

Scottish Law Online (2021) Scottish Law. [online] Available at: www.scottishlaw.org.uk (accessed 29 November 2021).

Slapper, G and Kelly, D (2009) *English Law*. Abingdon: Routledge-Cavendish.

Supreme Court Online (2021) The Supreme Court. [online] available at: www.supremecourt.uk (accessed 29 November 2021).

PART 1 LAW RELATING TO CHILDREN

3 Children at risk of significant harm

INTRODUCTION

This is the chapter most students will dread reading. Why? – because the minute you say children at risk of significant harm, students' brains go into overload and panic. How do you know that, you ask? Because when teaching this particular topic, as I look out into the crowd of students, I see the expressions on their faces change from excitement to dread and fear.

Remember, this book isn't about being a legal expert, but rather it is about giving you the knowledge of the law and how it applies to social work practice with children at risk of significant harm using a case study approach. It hopes to encourage you, the reader, to think about which aspects of the law apply to children who are both in need and at risk of significant harm and what your duties and responsibilities are within the statute. By using a case study, we will see how childcare legislation and their respective sections can be applied to Jane, a child that has come to your attention.

KEY LEGISLATION

Let us now consider the key legislation that relates to children at risk of significant harm. The Children Act 1989, I hear you all say. This is correct, but there are a few more pieces of legislation that apply, which are listed below. We all can quote the Children Act 1989 as one of the main pieces of legislation that social workers use. Despite being written in the 1980s, it is the equivalent to our 'Holy Grail'.

Definition of legislation (chronological order)

Children and Young Persons Act 1933

The oldest piece of child protection legislation, parts of which remain in force. The list of offences against children, referred to as schedule 1 offences, are set out in this Act.

The Children Act 1989

The Children Act 1989 underpins the work of children's services and social workers, providing a range of powers and duties to promote and protect the welfare of children and young people. It is underpinned by some key concepts and principles that all social workers will need to be familiar with and apply to their practice.

Education Act 2002

Section 175 requires all school governing bodies, local education authorities and further education institutions to make arrangements to safeguard children.

Children and Adoption Act 2006

This Act gives more flexible powers to facilitate and enforce contact orders (this means that any breaching of contact orders can be taken back to court and the order is varied, amended, or revoked) and extend family assistance orders as set out in section 16 of the Children Act 1989 (this relates to the court making an order requiring either a Cafcass officer or local authority officer to provide advice and assistance any person named in the order; these are used in a limited way) to 12 months.

Borders, Citizenship and Immigration Act 2009

Section 55 places a duty on the UK border agencies to safeguard and promote children's welfare in line with other public bodies.

HOW DO CHILDREN BECOME AT RISK OF SIGNIFICANT HARM?

When we look at the assessment framework for children in need (also referred to as the assessment triangle), there are three key areas where social workers assess need.

- o Child's developmental needs (including education, health, identity, emotional and behavioural development, family relationships, social relationships, self-care and social presentation).

- o Family and environmental factors (including community resources, social integration, income, employment, housing, wider family and family history and functioning).

- o Parenting capacity (including basic care, ensuring safety, emotional warmth, stimulation guidance and boundaries and stability).

These three factors are interlinked and dependent on each other. With the child at the heart of the assessment, any failure in parenting capacity can lead to delays or disruptions in the child's development. Any child developmental delay can result in a lack of ability to parent properly, while any family or environment factors can impact parenting capacity, which in turn impacts again on the child's development. This is represented in Figure 3.1.

The Act tells us that where a child is not meeting their developmental milestone or is unlikely to meet it, they are a child in need (CIN), but how does a child go from being in need to at risk of significant harm?

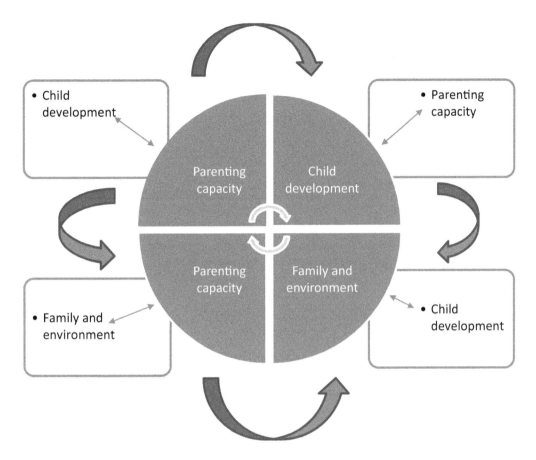

Figure 3.1 Interrelationship between child's developmental needs, family and environmental factors, and parenting capacity

Let's start at the very beginning, section 1 (1) of the Children Act, the welfare principle.

Welfare principle (section 1(1))

This refers to the courts' statutory duty to consider the child's welfare as the utmost consideration in any decisions involving the child's upbringing or property.

So, when the local authority has to decide about the child's welfare, with this being paramount, they will refer to the welfare checklist (Children Act 1989, s1(3)).

The welfare checklist

Section 1(3) of the Children Act outlines what the court uses as a checklist of welfare, which includes and is not limited to the following:

- the wishes and feelings of the child (ensuring that these are ascertained in an age-appropriate way);

- physical, emotional and educational needs;

- the impact of any change of circumstances on the child;

- a child's age, gender, background, and any other characteristic that can be considered of importance;

- any harm which the child has suffered or is at risk of suffering;

- the parent's ability to meet the needs of the child.

Now we are beginning to build a picture of the child's needs, in reference to the welfare checklist, and what happens when these needs are not met and how this may be defined within legislation. When these needs are not met, the local authority must then decide around the **harm** that the child may come to as a result of these unmet needs.

Children in need

The Children Act 1989 is not just about child protection; it also considers child welfare more generally and places a duty on local authorities to identify, assess and provide services for children, young people and families who meet the threshold to be considered in need (SCIE, 2012; National Society for the Prevention of Cruelty to Children, 2021).

'Children in need' is a term used to describe children and young people who may be experiencing social, economic or family difficulties, as well as those who may have additional or complex needs as a result of disability or other health issues.

Section 17: Child in need/family support

- This sets out the duty of every local authority to safeguard and promote the welfare of children who are in need in their area and, so far as is consistent with that duty, to promote the upbringing of these children by their families by providing support and services appropriate to the child's needs. A child in need is defined under section 17 as:

  - a child who is unlikely to achieve or maintain, or have the opportunity to do so, a reasonable standard of health or development without the provision of local authority services; or

  - a child whose health or development is likely to be significantly impaired, or further impaired, without the provision of local authority services; or

  - a child who is disabled.

Provision of services directly to the child, or to the family, can include:

- advice, guidance and counselling services;

- occupational, social, cultural or recreational activities;

o   family centres;

o   assistance in kind or in exceptional circumstances in cash;

o   direct payments/personal budgets;

o   accommodation.

DEFINING THE KEY SOCIAL WORK TERMS OF THE CHILDREN ACT 1989

Let us familiarise ourselves with the key terms used within the Children Act 1989 as these will become important in considering the case study.

o   Harm: ill treatment or the impairment of health or development, including sexual abuse and non-physical forms of ill treatment, eg being exposed to the ill treatment of someone else.

o   Significant harm: this is not defined in law, so the local authority threshold test determines if the significant harm threshold has been met. This is a very contentious issue in social care as different local authorities can define significant harm differently.

o   Health: relating to physical, emotional and mental health.

o   Development: relating to physical, intellectual, emotional, social or behavioural development.

These will be important considerations in relation to the case study of Jane and her sister Maria.

Case study

Jane is an eight year-old girl who is dual-heritage Asian and White British. She has a half-sibling Maria, who is ten years-old. Their mother, Saba (30), is in a relationship with Jason (38). Jane has recently disclosed to her youth worker that her mum is taking tablets with Jason and that she doesn't feed them because they both fall asleep after they take the tablets. Jane adds that once after taking the tablets, her mother got angry and started to throw things around the house. One of them hit her, cutting her left eye, and when she cried, Jason threatened to set her on fire so she would disappear forever while holding a lit match over her head. Maria has said (to the youth worker?) that she doesn't like Jason and is upset that her mother is not being a good mother to her and Jane and is picking Jason's side. Maria and Jane have different fathers, so Maria says she will go and live with her father but is worried that if she leaves Jane something bad will happen to her. Maria says she thinks that Jason hits Jane when she cries because she is hungry, but she is too scared to tell anyone.

DECISIONS MADE ON THE CASE

In the case of Jane, we need to determine if she and Maria need immediate protection.

Firstly, we need to determine if there is a risk to the life of Jane or the possibility of serious immediate harm. If so, one of the agencies with statutory child protection powers (the police and children's social care) should act quickly to secure the immediate safety of the children.

As we consider whether emergency action is required, we need to also consider whether action is required to safeguard and promote the welfare of other children in the same household (eg Maria).

If it is *necessary* to remove Jane and Maria from their home, the local authority must, where possible, apply for an emergency protection order (EPO, s44) unless Jane and Maria's safety is at immediate risk, in which case police powers or a Police Protection Order (PPO, s136) can be used in exceptional circumstances where there is not enough time to obtain an EPO or for reasons relating to the immediate safety of the child.

The strategy meeting

Planned emergency action will normally take place following an immediate strategy discussion/meeting between the police, children's social care, health professionals and other agencies as appropriate.

The strategy meeting determines that there is reasonable cause to suspect that Jane has suffered, or is likely to suffer, significant harm in the form of physical and emotional abuse and neglect. Jane and her sibling are at risk of significant harm and therefore a section 47 multi-agency assessment needs to take place immediately following the strategy discussion/meeting.

The local authority social worker has a statutory duty to lead enquiries under section 47 of the Children Act 1989. The police, health professionals, teachers and other relevant professionals should provide support in undertaking the enquiries.

The conclusions and recommendations of the section 47 enquiry should inform the assessment, which must be completed within 45 working days of the date when the referral was received.

Conducting a joint investigation

A joint investigation is conducted on behalf of Jane and her siblings as the allegations against Jason, if founded, could amount to a criminal offence against a child/minor. The police have established that an offence has been committed against the child and must therefore collect and process evidence to conduct a criminal investigation.

The police and children's social care must co-ordinate their actions to make sure the equivalent process of a section 47 enquiry and a criminal investigation is undertaken in the best interests of the child. This should primarily be achieved through joint activity and planning at the strategy discussions/meetings.

Where a case involves physical harm, the strategy discussions/meetings should where possible include the relevant clinician, where and when the child is to be seen or in urgent cases the duty paediatric team. For sexual assault cases, the strategy discussions/ meetings should include a paediatrician (for cases under 13 years) or a forensic nurse examiner (13 years and over).

Working Together to Safeguard Children (HM Government, 2018) states that:

> *The police should assist other agencies to carry out their responsibilities where there are concerns about the child's welfare, whether or not a crime has been committed. If a crime has been committed, the police should be informed by the local authority children's social care.*

> (HM Government, 2018, Chapter 2, section 11 of the Children Act 2004; updated December 2020 to include issues around contextual safeguarding)

Jane and Maria should be seen and communicated with alone by the social worker. All children within the household should be spoken with during section 47 enquiries by either the police or children's social care or both agencies, so as to enable an assessment of their safety to be made. As Jane is the focus of the main concern, she must be seen alone, subject to her age and willingness, preferably with parental permission. As the local authority social worker, it is the social worker's responsibility to ensure that appropriate actions are in place to support the child through the section 47 enquiry.

If Saba and Jason refuse access to Jane and Maria, then the social worker on the case, in consultation with their manager, should co-ordinate a strategy discussion/meeting including legal representation to develop a plan to locate or access the children and progress the section 47 enquiry.

Medical assessments should always be considered necessary where there has been a disclosure or there is a suspicion of any form of abuse to a child. The strategy discussion must consider the need for a medical assessment, which can take place for any one of the following reasons:

○ securing forensic evidence;

○ obtaining medical documentation;

○ providing reassurance for the child and parent;

○ informing treatment follow-up and review for the child (any injury, infection, new symptoms including psychological).

Only doctors can examine the whole child. All other staff should only note any visible marks or injuries on a body map and record, date and sign details in the child's file (Home Office, 2011).

Consent to examine a child or young person (under 16) must be obtained prior to undertaking a medical examination. You must be satisfied and the person giving consent be fully informed. It is the responsibility of the examining doctor to ensure that consent for the examination has been obtained.

Achieving best evidence interviews

Recorded interviews must be planned and conducted jointly by trained police officers and social workers in accordance with *Achieving Best Evidence in Criminal Proceedings: Guidance on Interviewing Victims and Witnesses, and Guidance on Using Special Measures* (Ministry of Justice, 2011).

So, a section 47 enquiry has taken place for Jane and Maria and the children are found to be at risk of significant harm from Jason and Saba, so the decision to remove the children to a place of safety has been made. The local authority convened a family group conference to consider family members and extended networks to care for the children (under private arrangements and connected persons) but no suitable person was found that could care for the children. It was determined that the children will be removed from the care of Saba and Jason under an EPO and placed in temporary foster placement until the assessment is completed and an Initial Child Protection Conference (ICPC) is convened.

Possible outcomes of the section 47 enquiries for Jane and Maria

The local authority is responsible for deciding how to proceed with the enquiries and risk assessment based on the strategy discussion/meeting and considering the views of Jane and her sibling, their parents and other relevant parties (eg a foster carer). It is important to ensure that both immediate risk assessment and long-term risk assessment are considered. Where Jane and her sibling's circumstances are about to change, the risk assessment must include an assessment of the safety of the new environment.

Once the section 47 enquiry is completed, children's social care must evaluate and analyse all the information gathered to determine if the threshold for significant harm has been reached.

There are three possible outcomes of the section 47 enquiry. These are that the original concerns are:

o not substantiated, although consideration should be given to whether the child may need services as a child in need;

o substantiated and the child is judged to be suffering, or likely to suffer, significant harm and an ICPC should be called;

○ disputed.

Concerns are not substantiated

If the concerns are not substantiated, then you must take the following actions:

○ discuss the case with the child, parents and other professionals and carefully determine whether support from any services may be helpful – if so, then help secure it;

○ consider whether the child's health and development should be re-assessed regularly against specific objectives and decide who has responsibility for doing this.

The team manager has the responsibility for authorising the decision on the case that no further action is necessary.

Concerns are substantiated

If concerns of significant harm are substantiated and the child is deemed to be suffering, or likely to suffer, significant harm there should be a convening of an ICPC. This should take place within 15 working days of a strategy discussion.

What happens in an Initial Child Protection Conference (ICPC)?

An ICPC should take place within 15 working days of the strategy discussion.

Where the child is unborn, then a pre-birth conference should take place. A pre-birth conference is an ICPC concerning an unborn child. Such a conference has the same status and purpose and must be conducted in an equivalent way to an ICPC.

At the ICPC, the social worker will bring together the family and all professionals working with them. This enables a multi-agency discussion of the main concerns, promotes sharing of information and assessment of the risk, and should result in putting a plan in place that is agreed by all. The aim is to always keep the welfare of the child at the centre of all the decisions made on the case while considering if the child is at continuing risk of significant harm (as identified by the strategy meeting and completed assessment).

All professionals must vote as to whether a child should be subject to a child protection plan. Please note that it is possible to go to an ICPC and for the professionals not to agree a child protection plan; in this situation it will be the independent reviewing officer who makes the final decision.

At the ICPC a date must be set for the first core group meeting, which must take place within ten days of the ICPC to review the plan.

Where the decision about the outcome of the section 47 enquiry is challenged

Where children's social care have concluded that an ICPC is not required following a section 47 enquiry but professionals in other agencies remain seriously concerned about the safety of a child, or if professionals disagree about any aspect of the enquiry at any other time, these professionals should seek further discussion with the social worker, their manager and/or the nominated safeguarding children adviser.

LOCAL AUTHORITY DUTIES AND RESPONSIBILITIES TO CHILDREN AT RISK OF SIGNIFICANT HARM

The powers and duties that frame the delivery of duties and powers under the Children Act 1989 are informed by three underlying principles:

- compulsory intervention in family life is to be minimised and practitioners should provide services;

- services should be provided to keep families together, only in so far as this safeguards and promotes the welfare of the child;

- the local authority should safeguard and promote the welfare of children in need and, so far as is consistent with that duty, they should promote the upbringing of such children by their families.

Duty to conduct section 47 enquiries

When the local authority social worker receives a referral and information has been gathered during an assessment (which may have been very brief), in the course of which a concern arises that a child may be suffering, or is likely to suffer, significant harm, the local authority is required by section 47 of the Children Act 1989 to make enquiries.

Responsibility for undertaking section 47 enquiries lies with the local authority children's social care in whose area the child lives or is found. 'Found' means the physical location where the child suffers the incident of harm or neglect (or is identified as likely to suffer harm or neglect), such as nursery or school, boarding school, hospital, one-off event such as a festival, holiday home or outing, or where a privately fostered or looked after child is living with their carers. For the purposes of this book, the local authority in which the child lives is referred to as the 'home authority' and the local authority children's social care in which the child is found is the child's 'host authority'. However, conversations can take place with the host authority and home authority as to which one will complete the enquiry if there are resource issues. This decision will be made at management level.

Key points to remember

Although there is a large amount of information contained within this chapter, the use of the case study should help to contextualise the law concerning section 47 (children at risk of significant harm).

The key thing to take away is that first you must establish if a child is at risk of harm. You do this using the information that is immediately available to you as the social worker. While this particular aspect of social work requires you to be able to make quick and effective decisions, you must always take a minute to think about your decision before rushing in. Remember, the local authority has a legal team who are available and on hand to give you advice. If in doubt, consult your legal team, line manager or senior manager.

If there is a concern about significant harm then a strategy meeting must take place, and a decision on how best to safeguard the child/ren must be made.

Ensure action is taken in a timely manner to avoid delays.

Speak to your supervisor/manager if you are in doubt.

I will leave you with this last thought that you can reflect on at the end of the chapter. Consider this: to what extent can the state interfere in an individual's family life? Many consider that there are ethical as well as human rights issues with this approach. When does care become control? What about positive risk taking? Should families be supported in taking risks?

TEST YOUR LEGISLATIVE KNOWLEDGE

Answers are at the back of the book.

Questions

- Is the promotion of 'well-being' a duty or a power?

- Outline three things the court considers as part of the welfare checklist.

- Is significant harm defined in law? What issues do you think this raises for local authorities?

- What three factors are considered in an assessment of children in need?

- Which section of the Children Act 1989 provides a definition of 'children in need'?

- Name two agencies that may be involved in a section 47 enquiry.

- What is an EPO and when can this be applied for?

- When is a PPO used?

CHAPTER SUMMARY

While often considered a complex aspect of social work, child protection requires a good understanding of child development, the law and family functioning. It is important to understand how family dynamics work and what risk factors can lead to a child becoming at risk of significant harm.

While significant harm is not defined in law, it is important that you familiarise yourself with the threshold criteria as this is what the court considers when making any orders – you can do this by speaking with your legal team who are able to offer you advice and guidance on possible options.

Our duties are clearly spelt out in the Children Act 1989 in relation to carrying out enquiries, making assessments, working with other professionals and safeguarding children. Decision making on serious harm cases are always seen as the most difficult to make, because it requires experience and skills to make sense of the information you have. Use the law to understand what steps you can take. Explore options with your manager; do not be risk averse, but rather use the information you have gathered and your professional judgement. Don't let your mind be clouded by the fear of making a wrong decision; seek support through supervision and discussion with your colleagues.

END OF CHAPTER ACTIVITY TO CAPTURE PERSONAL REFLECTIONS AND INDIVIDUAL THOUGHTS

Critically reflect on this chapter and what you have learned and record your own personal thoughts and feelings; use the mindmap to assist you. Also, as in previous chapters consider if there are any anti-discriminatory or anti-oppressive practice issues (Equality Act, 2010) that stand out for you.

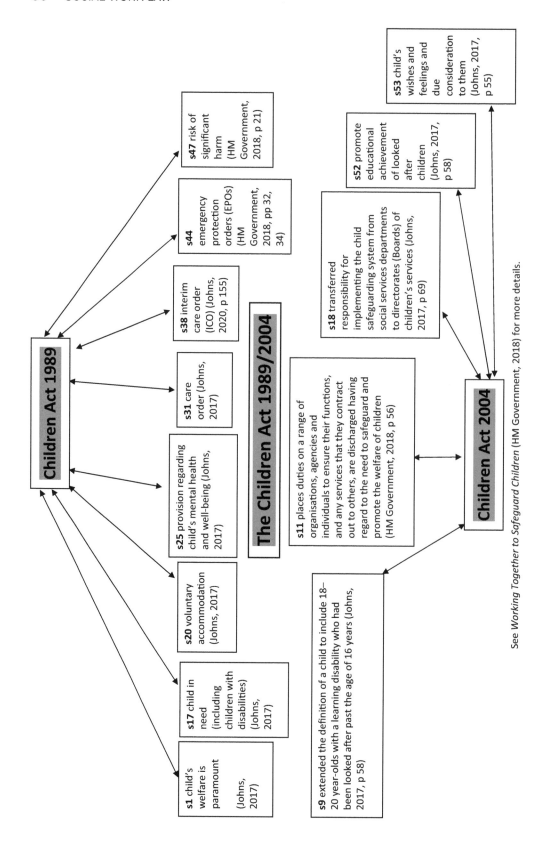

The Children Act 1989/2004

Children Act 1989

s47 risk of significant harm (HM Government, 2018, p 21)

s44 emergency protection orders (EPOs) (HM Government, 2018, pp 32, 34)

s38 interim care order (ICO) (Johns, 2020, p 155)

s31 care order (Johns, 2017)

s25 provision regarding child's mental health and well-being (Johns, 2017)

s20 voluntary accommodation (Johns, 2017)

s17 child in need (including children with disabilities) (Johns, 2017)

s1 child's welfare is paramount (Johns, 2017)

s9 extended the definition of a child to include 18–20 year-olds with a learning disability who had been looked after past the age of 16 years (Johns, 2017, p 58)

s11 places duties on a range of organisations, agencies and individuals to ensure their functions, and any services that they contract out to others, are discharged having regard to the need to safeguard and promote the welfare of children (HM Government, 2018, p 56)

s18 transferred responsibility for implementing the child safeguarding system from social services departments to directorates (Boards) of children's services (Johns, 2017, p 69)

s52 promote educational achievement of looked after children (Johns, 2017, p 58)

s53 child's wishes and feelings and due consideration to them (Johns, 2017, p 55)

Children Act 2004

See Working Together to Safeguard Children (HM Government, 2018) for more details.

Capture your personal reflections and individual thoughts here

REFERENCES

Children Act 1989 [online] Available at: www.legislation.gov.uk/ukpga/1989/41/contents (accessed 4 March 2022).

Equality Act 2010 [online] Available at: www.legislation.gov.uk/ukpga/2010/15/contents (accessed 4 March 2022).

HM Government (2018) *Working Together to Safeguard Children*. [online] Available at: https://assets.publishing.service.gov.uk/government/uploads/system/uploads/atta chment_data/file/942454/Working_together_to_safeguard_children_inter_agency_g uidance.pdf (accessed 7 March 2022).

Johns, R (2017) *Using the Law in Social Work*. 7th ed. London: Sage.

Johns, R (2020) *Using the Law in Social Work*. 8th ed. London: Sage.

Ministry of Justice (2011) Achieving Best Evidence in Criminal Proceedings: Guidance on Interviewing Victims and Witnesses, and Guidance on Using Special Measures. [online] Available at: www.cps.gov.uk/sites/default/files/documents/legal_guidance/best_ evidence_in_criminal_proceedings.pdf (accessed 25 April 2022).

National Society for the Prevention of Cruelty to Children (2021) Child Protection System in the UK. [online] Available at: https://learning.nspcc.org.uk/child-protection-system (accessed 13 December 2021).

Social Care Institute for Excellence (SCIE) (2012) Introduction to Children's Social Care. [online] Available at: www.scie.org.uk/publications/introductionto/childrenssocialcare/ childprotection.asp (accessed 13 December 2021).

4 When children become looked after

INTRODUCTION

This chapter will take you through the process of when children become looked after, accommodated or cared for in alternative arrangements. This is when the state intervenes in the removal or accommodation of children who are at risk of significant harm (you will remember this term from Chapter 3) or who have committed an offence.

The process of children coming into care is very procedural, but these procedures are embedded within specific childcare legislation that allow the state to step in and place children and young people into regulated placement either voluntarily (we will explore this further) or under an interim care order or care order.

Research over the years has highlighted the various factors associated with why children come into care, which include but are not limited to parental death, parental mental or ill health, substance misuse and domestic abuse. However, the local authority also considers the following factors.

o   Children who the court deem should no longer live within their own family. This could lead to a plan for permanence outside of the extended family. However, reintegration with their parents or a member of the extended family will be considered.

o   Children whose home situations have broken down and they have no alternative carers available within the extended family. For example, when a parent has died or gone into hospital or prison.

o   Children whose parents cannot control their behaviour at home, and this is causing risk to themselves and others.

o   Where a child has offended, and it is serious enough to warrant the court deciding that they should be looked after by children's social care rather than at home until the court process is concluded (Children Act 1989, s21).

The above considerations represent the two legal routes by which children become looked after. These can be referred to as voluntary – where a parent asks the local authority to look after their child for a short period of time to cover a family crisis (Children Act 1989, s20) or statutory – through a court process where the court decides that a child should be remanded as a result of committing a serious offence (Children Act 1989, s21) or a child is at risk of significant harm (Children Act 1989, s47) and planning needs to take place for their long-term care.

When families and children are unable to live together, planning should be dealt with quickly to identify a permanent and alternative setting. This is known as permanence planning.

The main difference between a child being in care and a child who is accommodated is that when a child is in care, the local authority as well as the parent has parental responsibility for the child. When a child is accommodated, the local authority does not have parental responsibility, only the parent does, and therefore decision making shifts in each scenario.

So, let us consider these processes within the context of a case study and look at how the law can be applied to the case study of ten year-old Mohammed.

Case study

Mohammed is a ten year-old boy who currently lives with his mother. She has been diagnosed with a terminal illness and has been given only months to live. Mohammed does not know his father and only has elderly grandparents that live in the local area with whom he stays when his mother is in hospital. At the moment the arrangements are working as it is a private agreement, but there is no long-term plan for the care of Mohammed. The local authority has intervened to support with the planning of Mohammed's long-term care.

KEY LEGISLATION FOR CHILDREN LOOKED AFTER

Within this case study, a good starting point is in understanding first which legislation applies to Mohammed, and second which gives the local authorities and the courts the powers and duty to act.

Children Act 1989

Section 1

Outlines that the welfare of the child is paramount; this is our starting point when considering our duties and actions taken in relation to the children in our care.

Section 21

The local authority shall make provision for accommodation for children in police protection or detention or on remand.

Sections 22A to 22D

Outlines that the local authority make provision for the accommodation and maintenance of a looked after child. They provide a framework within which decisions about the most appropriate way to accommodate and maintain the child must be considered.

Section 23

Outlines the duty for provision of accommodation and maintenance by the local authority for children whom they are looking after.

The Children Act 1989 guidance and regulations. Volume 2: care planning, placement and case review

Although not legislation, this is statutory guidance that the local authority must follow since it outlines duties at the heart of being a corporate parent. It highlights that the child should be at the centre of all work and decision making, that care planning is an effective process not only providing the child with accommodation but also meeting their needs and ensuring that a regular review mechanism is in place.

There are five volumes of guidance, and you can take a moment to familiarise yourself with some of the content of each one.

○ Volume 1 – Children Act 1989: court orders.

○ Volume 2 – Children Act 1989: care planning, placement and case review.

○ Volume 3 – Children Act 1989: transition to adulthood for care leavers.

○ Volume 4 – Children Act 1989: fostering services.

○ Volume 5 – children's homes regulations, including quality standards guide.

Care Standards Act 2000

This legislation covers the regulation of services and provisions of care providers, including the need for these services to be registered, be inspected and abide by a national minimum standard of care. This is relevant legislation because if Mohammed is placed into foster care, then there is a duty for the providers to comply with this legislation.

Adoption and Children Act 2002

The provisions of this Act deal with local authorities' duties to provide adoption services. The Act also covers the changes to parental responsibility after 2003. There was a drive to overhaul the existing Act of 1976, which was outdated. It aimed to align the provision of adoption law with the Children Act 1989 to ensure that the welfare principle was at its core in all adoption decisions. The Acts also provided for adoption orders to be made favourably to single people, married couples and unmarried couples.

Alongside the introduction of an independent mechanism for reviewing prospective adopters, it also implemented a new system for access to information held in adoption agency records and by the Register General about adoptions, which take place after the Act comes into force. Some of the key changes are summarised below.

○   To bring in new court rules governing the making of adoption orders and measures requiring the courts to draw up timetables for adoption cases to be heard. Freeing orders are now replaced by 'placement orders'.

○   To introduce a new special guardianship order for children for whom adoption is not a suitable option but who cannot return to their birth families.

○   To provide that an unmarried father can acquire parental responsibility for his natural child where he and the child's mother register the birth of their child together.

○   To introduce arrangements for stepfathers to acquire parental responsibility.

Children Act 2004

The main focus of this Act is to place a duty on agencies to work in partnership and share information. Section 10 covers co-operation to improve well-being and section 17 outlines the need for individual care plans for children to improve their well-being. These sections are relevant to Mohammed's case in relation to working together to ensure he has a plan for his long-term care that improves his well-being.

Children and Young Persons Act 2008

This Act introduced the ability for the local authority to delegate authority in relation to looked after children to those who provide social care services to children and, with this, the regulation of these providers requiring their registration under the Care Standards Act 2000 (part 2).

The Act gives clear guidance on the accommodation and care of children who are looked after and provides powers for additional provision in relation to the placement of looked after children by regulation. With this came a new mechanism for independent review of the decisions of fostering services who have identified that a prospective or existing foster parent is not suitable to foster.

The Act places a requirement on local authorities to take necessary steps to ensure that there is sufficient secure accommodation in their geographical area appropriate for the needs of the children they look after.

There were amendments to the duties of the local authority in relation to the appointment of independent reviewing officers (IROs) (Children and Young Persons Act 2008), adding to the functions of IROs, and providing powers for the relevant national authority to embed a new national IRO service independent of local authorities in England and Wales (section 42, Children and Young Persons Act 2008).

There was a new duty for local authorities to appoint an independent person to visit looked after children in their placements alongside the duty on local authorities to appoint an independent person to visit, befriend and advise any looked after child if doing so is in the child's interests.

The final important change was in relation to the rights of relatives who are entitled to apply for a child arrangement order (previously residence order) or special guardianship order without leave of the court to those with whom the child has lived for a continuous period of one year; and ensures that where a court makes a child arrangement order this lasts until the child reaches the age of 18 (section 43, Children and Young Persons Act 2008).

Children and Families Act 2014

The key provision in this Act relates to the amendment of the adoption process to ensure that it is made quicker, introducing the process of foster to adopt. Children have a new right to a quicker and more expedited process and must get more consideration in the legal system.

Children and Social Work Act 2017

The Children and Social Work Act 2017 (the Act) is intended to improve support for looked after children and care leavers, promote the welfare and safeguarding of children, and make provision for the regulation of social workers. The Act sets out corporate parenting principles for the local authority as a whole to be the best parent it can be to children in its care. These are largely a collation of existing duties local authorities have towards looked after children and those leaving care. Local authorities are required to publish their support offer to care leavers and to promote the educational attainment of children who have been adopted or placed in other long-term arrangements. The legislation extends the current considerations of the court when making decisions about the long-term placement of children to include an assessment of current and future needs and of any relationship with the prospective adopter (Children and Social Work Act 2017; Local Government Association, 2017).

In thinking about Mohammed, there are key decisions that need to be made about his long-term care, and the local authority's duties and powers are embedded within the legislation outlined above. Taking it from the first simple step, the decisions made are as follows.

DECISIONS MADE ON THE CASE/OPTIONS AVAILABLE IN RELATION TO MOHAMMED

Section 1 of the Children Act outlines the three principles that must be considered:

○   the welfare of the child is paramount;

○   delay is likely to prejudice the welfare of the child;

○   the court shall not make an order unless to do so would be better for the child than making no order (the 'no order' principle).

The key point of consideration here is that Mohammed cannot live with his mother as she is terminally ill, with only months to live. Therefore, under the Children Act 1989 Mohammed is a child in need (s17) in his local area. The local authority has a duty to ensure that those needs are met to promote his well-being, which in this case is one of accommodation and potential grief and loss. So, let's explore all of the options for Mohammed before a decision is made.

Staying or returning home

The first stage within planning for Mohammed's care is to support the work with families to ensure they stay together. The case study states that Mohammed currently lives at home with his mother; however, she is terminally ill, so this placement is not stable or able to be long term. While staying at home gives the best chance for stability for the child, research has proven that family preservation is a key factor for a higher success rate with reunification, which of course has to be balanced against the risks of harm to the child. However, as this is not possible for Mohammed, given that his mother has a terminal illness, the local authority has a duty to plan for the long-term care of Mohammed.

The first stage of this planning is to seek out all options, including placement with family and friends, and while doing this, the local authority can apply for an interim care order (section 38) that will allow them to have shared parental responsibility in order to make these decisions.

When undertaking permanence planning, it is extremely important to consider the child's culture, religion, heritage and race. However, this should not cause delay when achieving permanence for the child.

Friends and families (Regulation 24 connected persons)

If, after assessment, it is proved not safe for Mohammed to remain at home, every effort should be made to ensure a secure placement among relatives and/or friends or connected individuals such as his grandparents. This could be part of a plan to work towards the child returning home or, if a return home is not ideal or in the best interests of the child, it is very important to establish at an early stage relatives and/or friends who are available to care for that child to avoid unnecessary delays which are apparent during court proceedings.

Section 38: interim care order

An interim care order can be made if the court is satisfied reasonable grounds for a full care order (see below) have been met. It cannot be made *ex parte*, so parents must be informed of the application. Interim orders can last for up to eight weeks in the first instance to enable proceedings to be adjourned while investigations into the child's home circumstances take place.

Section 31: care order

A care order (s31(1)(a)) will place Mohammed into the care of the local authority and gives the local authority parental responsibility for the child. A parent does not cease to have parental responsibility in this situation, but the local authority will have the power to determine the extent to which a parent (or a guardian or special guardian or a step-parent) may exercise their parental responsibility. A care order can be made if the court is satisfied:

○ that a child is suffering or likely to suffer significant harm; *and*

○ this is attributable to the care given to the child not being what it would be reasonable to expect a parent to give; *or*

○ the child is beyond parental control.

An order lasts until the child is 18 years-old, or until an adoption, supervision, special guardianship or child arrangement order is made, or until the court decides the care order is no longer needed. The local authority or the child or any person with parental responsibility can apply for the order to be discharged (Children Act 1989, s39).

The planning process for permanency is informed by contributions from multiple agencies. They will identify which option of permanence is best to meet the needs of the individual child, also taking into consideration their feelings and wishes. It is imperative that the assessment process asks how stability will be finally achieved for the child. Having long-term stability ensures the child has a sense of a family unit and permanent home within their own community and culture. This will ensure continuity of relationships and identity for the child, whether it is short-term or medium-term stability; it is important for children who go to stay in care for a brief period before going home and for children who are going to need permanent placement arrangements.

You need to ensure educational experiences, links/contact with extended family, the child's hobbies and friendships alongside their support carer contribute to assist against disruption and placement breakdown.

It is important to listen carefully to what the child wants from their placement to help to build a great relationship between the child and their carer, and thorough plans around contact with the family, and to provide vigorous support during times of a crisis with a flexible attitude to adoption by carers.

The older the child, the less likely it is that they will secure a permanent family through adoption.

Long-term fostering

Long-term fostering is a provision of secure and stable care with a foster family who will care for a child or young person on a long-term basis; this will be until the child turns 18. Long-term foster care placements must be planned and regularly reviewed with care and a focus on the child or young person building positive, trusting relationships with the foster family (Fostering Network, 2021).

This option has been especially useful for older children who retain strong links to their birth families, children who do not want or need the formality of adoption and when the carer also wishes for the local authority to remain involved.

Special guardianship (section 14A)

A special guardian is someone who takes on the care of a child until they are 18 by applying for a special guardianship order via the court. A special guardianship order is relevant where a child requires a sense of security and stability within a placement away from their parents but without having an absolute legal break with their birth parents, as is associated with adoption rules and regulations. It also provides an alternative permanence in families where adoption, for cultural or religious reasons, is not an option.

Special guardians will have in place parental responsibility for the child until they are 18 but although this is shared among the children's parents, a special guardian is the one who has the legal right to make all day-to-day arrangements and decisions for that child. The parents will still have to be consulted with their consent required for a child to change name, be adopted or engage with a placement abroad for more than three months and any other fundamental issues which may follow with this.

A special guardianship order in relation to the child subject of a care order will automatically discharge that care order, meaning the local authority will no longer hold parental responsibility for that child.

While special guardianships may still be financially supported by the local authority, as with adoptive parents, they will also have the right to request an assessment for support services at any given time after the order has been made.

Adoption

Younger children are unable to be returned home where adoption is in place; a care order and placement order are usually necessary unless the parents are clearly relinquishing the child and agree with the plan or placement choice.

When adoption is not appropriate for a child, each case will need to be closely considered in terms of merits. The decision between special guardianship order, child arrangements order and long-term fostering under a care order will depend on the individual needs of the child.

Decision in relation to Mohammed

There is the option of care by his elderly grandparents, but this will need to be assessed to see if it is a viable placement. Remember in the first instance consideration should be made to keep children within their family and this includes their wider family (connected person). A viability assessment that is positive will allow his grandparents to be assessed for special guardianship (Children Act 1989, s1A). Consideration will need to be made about their ability to care for Mohammed until he is 18, whether their living accommodation is secure, and if they are able to care for him financially.

If following the special guardianship order assessment it is deemed that they are not able to do this, then the local authority, who would have applied for an interim care order as part of a parallel/twin planning process, would need to consider other connected persons or long-term fostering as an option.

LOCAL AUTHORITY DUTIES AND RESPONSIBILITIES TO LOOKED AFTER CHILDREN

Section 22(3) of the Children Act 1989 sets out the general duty of the local authority looking after a child to safeguard and promote their welfare. This duty underpins all activity by the local authority in relation to looked after children, and has become known as 'corporate parenting'. In simple terms, 'corporate parenting' refers to the collective responsibility of the council, elected members, employees and partner agencies for providing the best possible care and safeguarding for the children who are looked after by the council.

Section 22A imposes a duty on the responsible authority when a child is in their care to provide the child with accommodation.

Section 22B sets out the duty of the responsible authority to maintain a looked after child in other respects apart from providing accommodation.

Section 22C sets out the ways in which the looked after child is to be accommodated.

Section 22D imposes a duty on the responsible authority to formally review the child's case before making alternative arrangements for accommodation.

(Children Act 1989)

Key points to remember

- There are two legal routes for children to become looked after.

- The local authority as far as possible should try to keep the child within the family home with support.

- Where this is not possible, a plan should be made that involves extended family members to maintain that child's connections and identity and cultural needs.

- If the local authority is considering a placement outside of the extended family network, then a permanence plan must be considered.

TEST YOUR LEGISLATIVE KNOWLEDGE

Answers are at the back of the book.

Questions

- List three parental risk factors that may lead to a child becoming looked after.

- What are the legal routes to children becoming looked after?

- Name two orders that allow the local authority to plan for the long-term care of a child (these give them parental responsibility).

- Name three key pieces of legislation and how they relate to looked after children.

- What is family and friends care?

- What is an advantage of long-term fostering?

- Name at least one local authority duty to looked after children.

- What are the advantages of adoption?

CHAPTER SUMMARY

No parent wants their child to be removed from their care; after all, we have a right to a private and family life. However, there are occasions when parental risk factors or parental circumstances mean that a child cannot be cared for by their parents. In these situations, the local authority has a duty of care and duty to intervene to ensure that the appropriate steps are taken to safeguard the child/young person's well-being. This chapter has considered Mohammed and the circumstances that he finds himself in given his mother's terminal illness. Given that Mohammed is a child under the age of 18, the local authority has a duty to act to promote his well-being but to also plan for him to be cared for until he turns 18.

There are a number of options available to the local authority that will assist in their planning for the care of Mohammed, but they also need to consider the wider family network within their long-term plan for him. This can include family and friends/connected person care, special guardian, long-term fostering and adoption (if he was younger).

Mohammed's wishes and views would need to be sought throughout the process and his voice would be central to any decisions that the local authority takes. The role of the court in such processes is to consider the welfare of the child, to ensure that an order is only made if all options have been explored and that the process is a quick one and does not see children and young people dragged through proceedings that go on and on.

END OF CHAPTER ACTIVITY TO CAPTURE PERSONAL REFLECTIONS AND INDIVIDUAL THOUGHTS

Critically reflect on this chapter and what you have learned, recording your own personal thoughts and feelings; as in previous chapters, use the mindmap on page 36 to assist you. Also, as in previous chapters consider if there are any anti-discriminatory or anti-oppressive practice issues (Equality Act 2010) that stand out for you.

Capture your personal reflections and individual thoughts here

REFERENCES

Adoption and Children Act 2002 [online] Available at: www.legislation.gov.uk/ukpga/2002/38/contents (accessed 13 December 2021).

Care Standards Act 2000 [online] Available at: www.legislation.gov.uk/ukpga/2000/14/contents (accessed 13 December 2021).

Children Act 1989 [online] Available at: www.legislation.gov.uk/ukpga/1989/41/contents (accessed 4 March 2022).

Children Act 1989 Guidance and Regulations. Volume 2: Care Planning, Placement, and Case Review. [online] Available at: www.gov.uk/government/publications/children-act-1989-care-planning-placement-and-case-review (accessed 13 December 2021).

Children Act 2004 [online] Available at: www.legislation.gov.uk/ukpga/2004/31/contents (accessed 13 December 2021).

Children and Families Act 2014 [online] Available at: www.legislation.gov.uk/ukpga/2014/6/contents/enacted (accessed 13 December 2021).

Children and Social Work Act 2017 [online] Available at: www.legislation.gov.uk/ukpga/2017/16/contents/enacted (accessed 13 December 2021).

Children and Young Persons Act 2008 [online] Available at: www.legislation.gov.uk/ukpga/2008/23/contents (accessed 13 December 2021).

Equality Act 2010 [online] Available at: www.legislation.gov.uk/ukpga/2010/15/contents (accessed 7 March 2022).

Fostering Network (2021) [online] Available at: www.thefosteringnetwork.org.uk (accessed 13 December 2021).

Local Government Association (2017) *Get in on the Act: Children and Families Act 2014.* [online] Available at: www.local.gov.uk/sites/default/files/documents/get-act-children-and-fami-acf.pdf (accessed 13 December 2021).

Children in the criminal justice system

INTRODUCTION

While a history of the youth justice system would be a seemingly obvious starting point to a chapter on youth justice legislation, this book takes a different stance and presents a practical application of youth justice legislation to social work practice with children and young people using a case study approach. It hopes to encourage you, the reader, to think about which aspects of the law apply to children who offend, and what your duties and responsibilities are within the statute. By using a case study, you will see how different youth justice legislation can be applied to a young person who has been arrested and charged with offences by the police.

Let us start by thinking about when children and young people become criminally responsible. In the criminal justice system in England and Wales, a child or young person aged between 10 and 17 years must be treated as a youth. Anyone that is 18 years or older is an adult and treated as an adult within the criminal justice system.

In England and Wales, the age of criminal responsibility is defined as: *'[t]he age at which a child is deemed to be sufficiently "mature" to be held responsible before the substantive criminal law'* (Church et al, 2013, p 99). Therefore, a young offender is defined as someone under 18 years of age who has committed an offence. Given that the legal age of 'criminal responsibility' in England and Wales is ten years old, anyone therefore under the age of ten cannot be held criminally responsible for their actions (Arthur, 2012). While a child under ten cannot be charged with committing a criminal offence, they can however be given one of the following:

○ local child curfew (Crime and Disorder Act 1998, Part 1 (14));

○ child safety order (Crime and Disorder Act 1998, Part 1 (11)).

Children under the age of ten who break the law regularly can sometimes be taken into care, or their parents could be held responsible. A parent can be issued with a parenting order as a result of their child offending at such a young age (Crime and Disorder Act 1998, Part 1 (8)).

When young people first behave anti-socially or commit a minor offence (an offence is considered to be minor dependent on how serious it is, eg criminal damage), they can usually be dealt with by the police and local authority outside of the court system using a variety of orders and out-of-court disposals. This is to prevent young people from getting drawn into the youth justice system too early (Done, 2012; Kelly and Armitage, 2015); this process is often referred to as pre-court or out of court. When a young person offends and it is a serious offence, they enter into the youth justice system and interventions can be put in place to support them to desist from crime, which by large is the main aim of the youth justice system.

The Crime and Disorder Act 1998 outlined in statute that the main aims of the youth justice system are:

(1) *To prevent offending by children and young persons.*

(2) *In addition to any other duty to which they are subject, it shall be the duty of all persons and bodies carrying out functions in relation to the youth justice system to have regard to that aim.*

(Crime and Disorder Act 1998, Part 3 (37))

Within youth justice there are a number of key pieces of legislation that apply to or refer to children and young people, and they often cross reference one another. For example, the Children Act 1989 (s21) refers to the duties of the local authorities for provision of accommodation for children in police protection or detention or on remand.

First, we will look at the key legislation for young people who offend and then we will set these within the context of a case study while applying it to practice. This will enable you to consider sections within the legislation at a glance for easy reference. The key pieces of legislation in chronological order are:

○ Police and Criminal Evidence Act (PACE) 1984;

○ Crime and Disorder Act 1998;

○ Youth Justice and Criminal Evidence Act 1999;

○ Criminal Justice and Immigration Act 2008;

○ Legal Aid, Sentencing and Punishment of Offenders 2012.

DEFINITION OF LEGISLATION (CHRONOLOGICAL ORDER)

Police and Criminal Evidence Act (PACE) 1984

The Police and Criminal Evidence Act 1984 primarily focuses on the powers of the police in the execution of their duties. It covers such things as stop and search, arrest including issues around bail, detention and questioning and treatment of people by the police; it is relevant as it includes young people.

Crime and Disorder Act 1998

The Crime and Disorder Act 1998 was published on 2 December 1997. The primary areas were the introduction of anti-social behaviour orders, sex offender orders and parenting orders, allowing local authorities more responsibilities with regard to pol-icies for reducing crime and disorder, and the introduction of law specific to 'racially aggravated' offences. The Act also put an end to the rebuttable premise that a child is *doli incapax* (the assumption that a person between 10 and 14 years of age is incapable of committing an offence) and formally abolished the death penalty for the last offences carrying it, namely treason and piracy.

Youth Justice and Criminal Evidence Act 1999

The Youth Justice and Criminal Evidence Act 1999 (YJCEA) was introduced as part of New Labour's transformation of the youth justice system. This legislation introduced conditions in relation to children and young people, including referral orders and referral order panels.

Criminal Justice and Immigration Act 2008

Part 1 of the Criminal Justice and Immigration Act 2008 brought about reform in community sentences, positioning the sentencing options for youth in line with adult probation community orders. It introduced a new generic community sentence for children and young people (youth rehabilitation order, YRO). It set out the 'requirements' that may be attached to a YRO, made provision for their enforcement, revocation, amendment and transfer to Northern Ireland, and abolished certain existing community sentences which were replaced by the YRO. Pre-2008 community orders such as supervision orders, reparation attendance centre orders and curfew orders were stand-alone options available to the court when sentencing a young person to a community sentence. This took the nine community order options to one single option where requirements can be added to according to the assessed needs of the child or young person:

○ attendance centre;

○ activity requirement;

○ drug testing;

○ drug treatment;

○ education;

○ electronic monitoring;

○ exclusion;

○ curfew;

○ intoxicating substance treatment;

○ local authority residence;

○ mental health treatment;

○ programme requirement;

- prohibited activity;

- residence requirement;

- supervision;

- unpaid work;

- intensive fostering.

Legal Aid, Sentencing and Punishment of Offenders Act 2012

The Legal Aid, Sentencing and Punishment of Offenders Act 2012 (LASPO) saw a shift in direction relating to criminal proceedings. There are a number of changes that relate to young people, including:

- referral orders;

- bail amendments;

- remand to local authority accommodation;

- remand into youth detention accommodation;

- out-of-court disposals.

We will now consider the legislation outlined above within the context of a case study of a young man named Nitesh and explore how the law can be applied. This will include consideration of the possible options available to the professionals involved in relation to their duties and responsibility for a child under 18 who has offended.

Case study

Nitesh is 16 years-old and has been drinking alcohol for the last three years. Having been excluded from school at 15 years of age, Nitesh is currently not in education, training or employment. Recently, Nitesh has started associating with a group of older youths who are involved in offending. This is the first time that Nitesh has got into trouble with the police.

Nitesh's parents have become increasingly concerned about him and are now at their wits' end because Nitesh has been arrested for the following offences:

- robbery;

- possession of an offensive weapon (pocketknife);

- possession of cannabis.

The principal focus of this case study is on the application of the law in relation to the youth justice processes. So, we will take each stage that relates to Nitesh from when he is arrested to when he exits the court process into either the community or custody.

The case study raises a number of issues for Nitesh, the first being his age and the second being the seriousness of the offences that he has committed. The offence of robbery is classified as a specified offence, or a schedule 15 offence (Criminal Justice Act 2003); this means an offence which is punishable by imprisonment of 14 years or more if committed by an adult. These offences are often violent or of a sexual nature.

As these are Nitesh's first offences, it is important to explore the options available to him as a young person who has offended. While at the police station as a young person under 17, he should be accompanied by an appropriate adult during interview. This can be either a parent/carer, an appropriate adult service or a local authority social worker (PACE Act 1984 and Crime and Disorder Act 1998). The appropriate adult's role is to ensure that the welfare of the child is considered and to protect their best interests; it is also to support and advise as well as to ensure their rights are upheld. An appropriate adult must always be present if a child or young person is charged.

Children have a number of rights while in police custody, which are safeguarded under the provisions in the United Nations Convention on the Rights of the Child. Article 37 (b) states that:

> No child shall be deprived of his or her liberty unlawfully or arbitrarily. The arrest, detention or imprisonment of a child shall be in conformity with the law and shall be used only as a measure of last resort and for the shortest appropriate period of time.

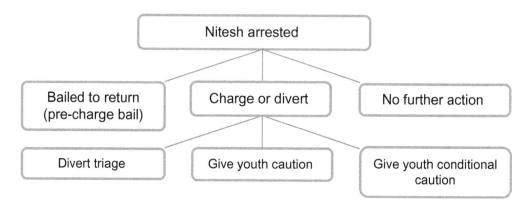

Figure 5.1 The possible options for Nitesh at the police station

Following Nitesh's arrest and presentation at the police station, the police have a number of options available to them to deal with Nitesh (see Figure 5.1).

If Nitesh is bailed to return, he will be given bail conditions to adhere to until he has to return to the police station on a given date by the officer in the case (OIC). Often bail is issued pending further investigations or waiting on evidence (PACE 1984, Part 4 (47)).

The decision whether to charge Nitesh will be made by the police dependent on the seriousness of the offence, an omission of guilt and if it is a first offence. If Nitesh is charged, the options are as follows if the police want to divert him from court:

○ youth caution;

○ youth conditional caution.

Prior to LASPO, the police had powers to give cautions and final warnings. Under LASPO (2012 section 135), the law states that:

> *(1) A constable may give a child or young person ('Y') a caution under this section (a 'youth caution') if—*
>
> > *(a) the constable decides that there is sufficient evidence to charge Y with an offence,*
> >
> > *(b) Y admits to the constable that Y committed the offence, and*
> >
> > *(c) the constable does not consider that Y should be prosecuted or given a youth conditional caution in respect of the offence.*
> > (Legal Aid, Sentencing and Punishment of Offenders Act 2012)

The police have the option of no further action should there be insufficient evidence to charge (a charging decision is sent to the evidence reviewing officer [ERO] for a decision or referral to the Crown Prosecution Service [CPS]).

As we have determined earlier, the offence of robbery is a specified offence (meaning an offence which is punishable by imprisonment of 14 years or more if committed by an adult), meaning that Nitesh will be charged despite him admitting guilt and it being his first offence as it is a serious offence. The police will refer the matter to the Youth Court and may impose bail conditions on Nitesh (either with conditions known as *conditional bail* or without conditions known as *unconditional bail*). Nitesh will then be remanded on bail to appear in court. On occasion the police may keep Nitesh in custody overnight if the next Youth Court sits the following day – this ensures that Nitesh is processed quicker. If there is also no bail address available for Nitesh, the police may keep Nitesh overnight until a bail address is found or he is remanded on bail to local authority accommodation (see Figure 5.2).

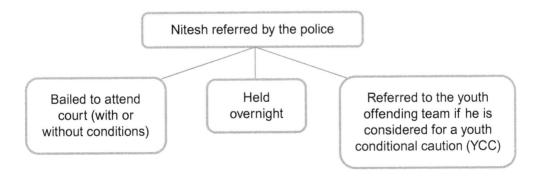

Figure 5.2 Options available to the police at this stage of the process

Nitesh is remanded on conditional bail and set to appear before the Youth Court the following week.

What happens in the Youth Court?

Nitesh will appear at the first available date for the Youth Court and will have an opportunity to enter his plea (often referred to as a pleas and directions hearing) in front of a judge or a magistrate (lay bench, which refers to magistrates who are not legally trained). Each local authority youth offending team (YOT) will have a representative known as a court officer present when a child or young person is in court. Their role is to advise the court if the young person is already known to them or social care. It is also to assess the young person for a bail supervision and support package if a bail application is made by their legal representative (solicitor).

At court, the options available will be based on it being Nitesh's first offence and what plea he enters.

As this is Nitesh's first offence and he has entered a guilty plea, under the Youth Justice and Criminal Evidence Act 1999 he will be eligible for a youth referral order, absolute discharge, or conditional discharge (Youth Justice and Criminal Evidence Act 1999, Part 1, s1–5).

o   A referral order is available for all young people aged 10–17.

o   It must be imposed on any youth with no previous convictions who pleads guilty to any imprisonable offence unless the court is considering an absolute discharge, conditional discharge, Mental Health Act order or custody.

o   The length of the order must be for a minimum of three months and a maximum of 12 months.

o   The order runs from the date the contract is signed (not the court date).

o   The court must order a parent/guardian to attend the meetings of the youth offender panel, where the youth is 10–15 years old, and may order parental attendance for those aged 16–17. Failure to attend a panel meeting may result in the parent being brought back before the court.

Where the court sentences someone to an absolute discharge, it will be because the offence is minor and a punishment is not warranted given particular factors relating to the defendant or their individual/personal circumstances, which justify such a course of action.

A conditional discharge is more serious; however, the judge/magistrate does not consider that the punishment needs to be given immediately. It requires the defendant to not commit an offence for a period of up to three years maximum. If an offence is committed within the specified time period (determined by the judge/magistrate), then they will return to court and be resentenced for the original offence along with the breach of the conditional discharge.

Let us explore further options for Nitesh if he pleads not guilty when he attends court. A trial date will be set under the provisions of the Crime and Disorder Act 1998. Nitesh's solicitor will apply for bail for Nitesh, and if granted by the court bail conditions will be imposed on Nitesh while he awaits his trial. The court also has the powers to remand Nitesh to local authority accommodation (often referred to as RILAA) or into custody (young offenders' institute). The court has the powers to remand Nitesh into custody pending trial based on the following:

o   the seriousness of the offence;

o   impact on victim and any associated risks to victim/witness intimidation;

o   no suitable bail address.

If Nitesh is instead remanded on bail and released pending trial, he will need to adhere to either bail conditions which may involve reporting to the police station, or a bail supervision and support package provided by the local youth offending team (YOT) in the area in which he resides.

Youth court trial

If found guilty at trial, the court will request the local YOT to prepare a pre-sentence report (PSR – as defined by the Criminal Justice Act 2003) within three weeks for sentencing.

If found not guilty at trial, the case will be closed and all charges will be dropped against Nitesh.

Given that Nitesh has attended court and pleads guilty to the offences of robbery and possession of an offensive weapon, the court has the power to sentence him. In sentencing a young person, the Sentencing Council of the United Kingdom (2017) states the following:

> When sentencing children or young people (those aged under 18 at the date of the finding of guilt) a court must have regard to:
>
> o   the principal aim of the youth justice system (to prevent offending by children and young people), and
>
> o   the welfare of the child or young person.

While the seriousness of the offence will be the starting point, the approach to sentencing should be individualistic and focused on the child or young person, as opposed to offence focused. For a child or young person, the sentence should focus on rehabilitation where possible. A court should also consider the effect the sentence is likely to have on the child or young person (both positive and negative) as well as any underlying factors contributing to the offending behaviour.

What happens post court

Now that Nitesh has pleaded guilty, given that it is his first offence he is eligible for a referral order and the court sentences him to a 12-month referral order. Once sentenced, Nitesh will be referred to the YOT for supervision under the provision of the Criminal Justice and Immigration Act 2008, Part 1 (1) and Part 2 (9). Nitesh would be supervised by his local YOT for the duration of his order.

DECISIONS MADE ON THE CASE STUDY

It is important to know how the law has been applied to Nitesh and how decisions are made in relation to its application to Nitesh. You will see that very few decisions are made about Nitesh by the local authority or YOT worker until Nitesh is arrested and attends court. The balance that the professionals have to make at all stages is in relation to section 1 of the Children Act 1989 (the welfare principle); when considerations need to be made, this should take into account the young person's welfare and individual circumstances while promoting public protection. At the pre-court stage, the decisions, and powers in law rest with the police and YOT.

To enable you to see how the decision was made in relation to Nitesh, the following was considered.

○   Youth justice legislation always considers the age of the child (Crime and Disorder Act 1998; Youth Justice and Criminal Evidence Act 1999; Criminal Justice and Immigration Act 2008; Legal Aid, Sentencing and Punishment of Offenders 2012). Nitesh is 16, which means he must be treated as a child and is subsequently covered by the UN Convention on the Rights of the Child, and the Children Act 1989 (welfare principle).

○   Consideration needs to be made in relation to Nitesh's ability to understand what is happening to him and his personal circumstances.

○   How serious these offences are will determine whether a charge will be brought against him by the police or CPS (Nitesh has committed three offences and has been charged with these offences).

Key points to remember

If working with a child or young person who commits an offence, consider if it is their first offence; think about whether this is Nitesh's first offence. If it is the first offence, the options available to the child/young person would be different than if they have previous convictions; it would also depend on what those previous convictions are. For example, if Nitesh has previous offences the YOT will need to consider why Nitesh is offending; if Nitesh commits three or more offences and is convicted of them within a 12-month period the law sees him as a persistent young offender. This will increase Nitesh's likelihood of getting a custodial sentence.

Children who get in trouble for the first time or for less serious offences can be dealt with informally by the police. If a child is interviewed and admits to doing something wrong, the police should always consider out-of-court disposals: triage, community resolution or youth cautions. Triage is recorded on the police national computer (PNC) as no further action (NFA).

DUTIES AND RESPONSIBILITIES TO YOUNG OFFENDERS

In this section, we will focus on the duties and responsibilities of the local authority and the local authority officer in relation to the outlined legislation.

Crime and Disorder Act 1998, Part 3, section 37

States that each local authority shall make provisions of youth justice services.

Crime and Disorder Act 1998, Part 3, section 39

States that every local authority must have a YOT with officers who are responsible for the supervision and management of young offenders. This places a duty on the local authority towards children who offend via the YOT. Often seen as separate to children's social care, YOTs are specialist teams who work with young people who offend to supervise and support them to desist from offending. They complete a comprehensive assessment of needs and make plans to supervision children both in the community and within the secure estate or young offenders' institute. Currently YOT officers do not need to be qualified social workers but must demonstrate a clear understanding of children who offend and have some knowledge of the law.

So, returning to the case study of Nitesh, he has now unfortunately found himself in trouble with the law and has gone through a process of arrest to receiving a referral order where he will be supervised by his local YOT to rehabilitate and prevent further recidivism. Let us now test your knowledge based on what you have learned in this chapter.

TEST YOUR LEGISLATIVE KNOWLEDGE

Answers are at the back of the book.

Questions

- Name three pieces of legislation that relate to young people who offend.

- What is the principal aim of the youth justice system?

- Which Act brought about the formation of the Youth Justice Board and the youth offending teams?

- At what age is a child criminally responsible in England and Wales?

- Which 2008 Act brought about a reform of sentences for young people?

- What is the name of the community order that was introduced for youth in 2008?

- Name three requirements that could be added to a youth rehabilitation order.

- Which two Acts refer to appropriate adults?

- What is a specified offence? (Schedule 15 offence)

CHAPTER SUMMARY

Youth justice is always thought about outside of specific social work training, skills and qualifications, and as such is considered a specialism. This chapter has considered various pieces of youth justice legislation and its direct application to practice by considering the case study of Nitesh. Although this is a case study, the principles considered could apply in a practice situation within a youth offending team. The case study was considered in relation to how decisions were made in line with the relevant legislation and its application to children who offend and what options were available.

Before considering the next chapter which focuses on the Mental Capacity Act 2005, we would like to end this chapter by encouraging you to record your personal reflections and individual thoughts; you may like to write them directly into this book to keep for future reference.

END OF CHAPTER ACTIVITY TO CAPTURE PERSONAL REFLECTIONS AND INDIVIDUAL THOUGHTS

Critically reflect on this chapter and what you have learned and record your own personal thoughts and feelings. Also, as in previous chapters consider if there are any anti-discriminatory or any anti-oppressive practice issues (Equality Act 2010) that stand out for you, particularly in relation to the UN Convention on the Rights of the Child and the Human Rights Act 1998.

Capture your personal reflections and individual thoughts here

REFERENCES

Arthur, R (2012) Rethinking the Criminal Responsibility of Young People in England and Wales. *European Journal of Crime, Criminal Law and Criminal Justice*, 20(1): 13–29.

Children Act 1989 [online] Available at: www.legislation.gov.uk/ukpga/1989/41/contents (accessed 4 March 2022).

Church, R, Goldson, B and Hindley, N (2013) The Minimum Age of Criminal Responsibility: Clinical, Criminological/Sociological, Developmental and Legal Perspectives. *Youth Justice*, 13(2): 99–101.

Crime and Disorder Act 1998 [online] Available at: www.legislation.gov.uk/ukpga/1998/37/contents (accessed 4 March 2022).

Criminal Justice Act 2003 [online] Available at: www.legislation.gov.uk/ukpga/2003/44/contents (accessed 9 March 2022).

Criminal Justice and Immigration Act 2008 [online] Available at: www.legislation.gov.uk/ukpga/2008/4/contents (accessed 4 March 2022).

Done, F (2012) Youth Cautions: Keeping Children Out of Court. *Criminal Law and Justice Weekly*, 176(47): 678.

Human Rights Act 1998. [online] Available at: www.legislation.gov.uk/ukpga/1998/42/contents (accessed 4 March 2022).

Kelly, L and Armitage, V (2015) Diverse Diversions: Youth Justice Reform, Localized Practices, and a 'New Interventionist Diversion'? *Youth Justice*, 15(2): 117–33.

Legal Aid, Sentencing and Punishment of Offenders Act 2012 [online] Available at: www.legislation.gov.uk/ukpga/2012/10/contents/enacted (accessed 4 March 2022).

Police and Criminal Evidence Act 1984 [online] Available at: www.legislation.gov.uk/ukpga/1984/60/contents (accessed 4 March 2022).

Sentencing Council of the United Kingdom (2017) Sentencing Children and Young People. [online] Available at: www.sentencingcouncil.org.uk/overarching-guides/magistrates-court/item/sentencing-children-and-young-people (accessed 4 March 2022).

United Nations Convention on the Rights of the Child (2022) [online] Available at: www.unicef.org/child-rights-convention (accessed 9 March 2022).

Youth Justice and Criminal Evidence Act 1999 [online] Available at: www.legislation.gov.uk/ukpga/1999/23/contents (accessed 4 March 2022).

PART 2 LAW AFFECTING CHILDREN AND ADULTS

6   Mental Capacity Act 2005

INTRODUCTION

In this chapter, the Mental Capacity Act (MCA) 2005 will be considered in the context of application to practice with adults and when a child is transitioning from child to adult services using a case study approach; as used in some previous chapters there is also a mindmap for you to refer to, to enable you to consider sections within the MCA 2005 at a glance for easy reference. There were amendments to the MCA 2005 in 2009, which resulted in the Deprivation of Liberty Safeguards (DoLS), and in 2019, which resulted in the Liberty Protection Safeguards (LPS) that are targeted to replace DoLS in April 2022, but these will be considered in the next chapter; this chapter will focus on the MCA 2005. As with previous chapters, additional legislation will be indicated in brackets to encourage you to conduct your own further research and become familiar with other legislation and guidance.

The MCA applies to all people over the age of 16 years (Johns, 2020) who live in England and Wales and who may lack the capacity (within s2(1)) to make all or some decisions for themselves. It provides the legal framework to assess whether an individual can make decisions for themselves and, if they lack capacity, to facilitate a plan of action to act in the person's best interests (s4). The purpose of the MCA is to put people at the centre of making their own decisions (SCIE, 2016) to enable promotion of choice and autonomy while also being supported by decision makers such as a carer responsible for day-to-day care, social worker, doctor or nurse to ensure that decisions are made in the individual's best interests (s1, Principle 4, s4).

The MCA 2005 received Royal Assent on 7 April 2005 and the Act clarified the way decisions were to be made on behalf of others:

> *The Act will govern decision-making on behalf of adults, both where they lose mental capacity at some point in their lives, for example as a result of dementia or brain injury, and where the incapacitating condition has been present since birth. It covers a wide range of decisions, on personal welfare as well as finan-cial matters and substitute decision-making by attorneys or court-appointed 'dep-uties', and clarifies the position where no such formal process has been adopted. The Act includes new rules to govern research involving people who lack capacity and provides for new independent mental capacity advocates to represent and provide support to such people in relation to certain decisions. The Act provides recourse, where necessary, and at the appropriate level, to a court with power to deal with all personal welfare (including health care) and financial decisions on behalf of adults lacking capacity.*
>
> (MCA 2005 Explanatory Notes)

Next, the case studies of Liliani, Alexander and Lydia will be considered in the context of the MCA 2005: Liliani and Alexander in the context of adult application of the MCA 2005 and Lydia in the context of a child transitioning to adult services.

Case study

Alexander aged 78 and Liliani aged 76 have been together for 30 years. Alexander has become increasingly concerned about Liliani as he has been noticing that Liliani has become very forgetful, including forgetting to eat. One day, Liliani ventures out in the middle of the night wearing just her nightie. Alexander notices Liliani has gone and calls the police, who find Liliani wandering the streets.

The case study raises some questions, such as: how does the MCA 2005 support and safeguard Liliani? How would Liliani be assessed to see if she has capacity? If Liliani is deemed to lack capacity, how could the least restrictive option be applied? In this chapter you will be provided with knowledge and guidance to enable you to apply the MCA 2005 in practice.

THREE PARTS TO THE MCA 2005

There are three parts to the MCA 2005; Part 1 covers persons who lack capacity (s1–s62) and includes:

○   the five principles (s1);

○   two-stage test (s2, s3);

○   best interests (s1 Principle 4, s4);

○   lasting power of attorney (s9);

○   lasting power of attorney restrictions (s11);

○   appointment of deputies (s19);

○   advance decisions (s24–s26);

○   Independent Mental Capacity Advocate service (s35–s41).

Part 2 covers:

○   the Court of Protection and the Public Guardian (s45–s63);

○   Court of Protection (s45–s46);

○   application to the Court of Protection (s50);

○   the Public Guardian (s57–s60).

Part 3 covers miscellaneous and general (s62–69), for example the scope of the Act (s62).

While as a social worker it is not necessary to commit to memory the entire content of the MCA 2005, it is important to remember key aspects of it to enable best practice when working with people who may or may not lack capacity; for the purpose of this chapter, the starting point of the MCA will be the five principles within section 1 (s1).

FIVE PRINCIPLES UNDER THE TERMS OF THE MCA

The MCA provides the legal framework to assess whether an individual can make decisions for themselves or, if they lack capacity, to facilitate a plan of action to act in the person's best interests (s1 Principle 4, s4). Under the terms of the MCA section 1, there are five principles.

Principle 1

Assume capacity unless it is established the person does not have capacity; this could be permanent lack of capacity or temporary. Under this principle, individuals are also protected in terms of protective characteristics which are personal to the individual and could include age, gender, ethnicity, class, appearance (for example, if someone presents as dishevelled), disability or impairment. When applying this principle to the case study, this would mean that initially Liliani would be assumed to have capacity, even if her behaviour indicates otherwise, until a two-stage test had been undertaken to establish whether she does or does not have capacity (s2, s3).

Principle 2

A person is not treated as unable to make a decision unless all practicable steps have been taken without success, so everything possible must be done to try to support the person; for example, if someone is non-verbal then language support should be put in place. Liliani would be supported and encouraged to engage meaningfully in decision making. She could be supported by family such as her husband Alexander or, if she did not want Alexander to support her, it could be a friend or an advocate.

Principle 3

A person is not to be treated as unable to make a decision merely because he/she makes an unwise decision. However, how would an unwise decision be defined? An unwise decision could be a personal decision, such as a diet choice of whether to eat meat or be vegan; both decisions could be deemed to be wise or unwise depending on the individual's personal choice. Although it could be argued that Liliani going out in the middle of the night in just a nightie could be deemed an unwise decision, it is not to be immediately considered an unwise decision because it could be argued everyone makes unwise decisions, such as buying an item of clothing in the sale because it was a bargain even though it was two sizes too small.

Principle 4

Best interests cannot be determined on the grounds of age, appearance as indicated above when considering protective characteristics (Principle 1) or behaviour. You must consider, so far as reasonable, the person's a) past and present wishes and feelings, b) beliefs and values that would influence the decision if the person had capacity, and c) other factors the person would likely consider if they were able to do so. Therefore, in this case if conducting an assessment (s2, s3; NICE, 2021), it needs to be ascertained what Liliani's views were prior to her forgetfulness, perhaps, for example, by talking to her family and friends.

Principle 5

When you are restricting a person's freedom, you need to ensure you safeguard while carrying out the least restrictive option. Part of identifying the least restrictive option is communicating with individuals at times they can communicate better, perhaps earlier in the morning, to find out their wishes, views and feelings. Staff, carers' and family's input is also essential as the combined contribution can find a solution to keep the individual safe while still restricting freedom as little as possible (Griffiths, 2012). For example, consider a person with dementia, which affects memory and thinking (Dementia UK, 2021), and requires care and support; what would be the least restrictive option while still keeping the person safe? It could be admittance to a psychiatric unit but this could be deemed too restrictive for this person individually, so the least restrictive option could be a nursing home. Principle 5 will be considered in greater detail with regard to Liliani, after considering the two-stage test.

TWO-STAGE TEST

If a person's capacity is tested, it is done so by undertaking a two-stage test to determine if someone lacks capacity (s2, s3). First, it needs to be established whether the person has a permanent impairment (such as a brain injury) or a temporary disturbance (such as substance misuse) in the functioning of the mind or brain (s2). Second (s3), it needs to be determined if a person is unable to make a decision for themselves if they are unable to:

○ understand information relevant to a decision;

○ retain that information;

○ use or weigh up information as part of the process of making the decision or needs.

Communication support to make the decision would need to be provided, which would include an interpreter if required (s3).

If a person is considered to lack capacity, although decisions may be made for them, it always has to be in the person's best interests, so for example if you knew the person was a strict vegetarian prior to lacking capacity, these choices should be upheld after they are assessed as lacking capacity.

Going back to the case study, Liliani has now undergone the two-stage test (s2, s3) and was deemed to lack capacity. She has also undergone testing to see if she has a neurological condition and has been diagnosed with advanced Alzheimer's disease, a genetic/hereditary condition that affects memory, thinking and behaviour (Alzheimer's Association, 2020). Although Liliani lacks capacity, section 1, Principle 5 emphasises that whatever decisions are made need to be '*the least restrictive option whilst balancing best interest with risk*'. For example, if Alexander was finding Liliani's behaviour difficult and needed support to care for her, what would be best for Liliani and also Alexander: a psychiatric hospital, a care home or care at home? Alexander says he can manage with carers as he is now retired, Liliani wants to stay at home and Alexander wants to try and provide care and support for his wife; thus, this option would be considered.

The least restrictive option would be to receive care in her home but this may not be in Liliani's best interests due to welfare/safety concerns that Liliani may wander off in the night again. The least restrictive, safer option could be a nursing home, which allows her more freedom and a less restrictive regime than a psychiatric unit, but has more supervision than she would receive at home.

Although we have considered the five principles (s1) and the two-stage test (s2, s3), in terms of the case study the MCA is important because a person's mental capacity could be affected at any stage in their life, due to accident, trauma, stroke (blood supply to part of the brain is cut off) or degenerative conditions such as dementia, Alzheimer's disease (genetic/hereditary – affects memory, thinking and behaviour; Alzheimer's Association 2020; Goldman et al, 2008) and Huntingdon's disease (a hereditary disease marked by degeneration of the brain cells and causing chorea, which are involuntary movements and progressive dementia, which affects memory and thinking; Goldman et al, 2008; Dementia UK, 2021), to name but a few. Social workers need to understand the law to support the people with whom they are working.

BEST INTERESTS

The Mental Capacity Act 2005 Code of Practice (2007, 5.13) sets out a best interest for decision-making checklist to support the best interest process (SCIE, 2014; Council for Disabled Children, 2015).

SCIE (2014, p 1) highlight that:

> The '*best interest*' principle underpins the Mental Capacity Act. It is set out in chapter 5 of the MCA Code and states that: An act done, or decision made, under this Act for or on behalf of a person who lacks capacity must be done, or made, in his best interests.

When considering the best interests of a person, also consider difference and diversity, for example beliefs and cultural values (s1, Principle 4). So when considering Liliani, have her personal values, beliefs, wishes and feelings been taken into consideration? As Liliani has been assessed as lacking capacity, in the future, if her condition deteriorates, she may need to be cared for in a care home; therefore, knowledge and understanding of her individuality could make a difference in her care, support and protection.

Carr and Goosey (2017, p 484) posit that the MCA 2005 is:

> Designed to ensure that the wishes of the service user are taken into account as far as is possible, and where that is not possible, to set in place mechanisms to ensure that the best interests of the service user are protected.

In determining for the purposes of this Act what is in a person's best interests, the person making the determination must not make it merely on the basis of:

(a) the person's age or appearance; or

(b) a condition of the person, or an aspect of their behaviour, which might lead others to make unjustified assumptions about what might be in the person's best interests (s1, Principle 4).

So far as is reasonably ascertainable:

(a) the person's past and present wishes and feelings (and, in particular, any relevant written statement made by them when they had capacity) must be taken into consideration;

(b) consider the beliefs and values that would be likely to influence the person's decision if they had capacity;

(c) examine the other factors that the person would be likely to consider if they were able to do so.

It must be taken into account, if it is practicable and appropriate to consult them, the views of:

(a) anyone named by the person as someone to be consulted on the matter in question or on matters of that kind;

(b) anyone engaged in caring for the person or interested in their welfare;

(c) any donee (person appointed by an individual to handle their affairs if they no longer have capacity) of a lasting power of attorney (LPA) granted by the person;

(d) any deputy appointed for the person by the court, as to what would be in the person's best interests.

For more information see MCA 2005.

So, consulting people that can inform you to be able to make the best decision in the person's best interest is essential.

In summary, if a person has been assessed as lacking capacity (s2, s3), then any action taken, or any decision made for or on behalf of that person, must be made in his or her best interest (s1, Principle 4, s4).

THE ROLE OF THE INDEPENDENT MENTAL CAPACITY ADVOCATE

An Independent Mental Capacity Advocate (IMCA) must be appointed to anyone 16 years or over where serious medical treatment or a change of residence is proposed for a person who lacks capacity and where that person has no family or friends whom it is appropriate to consult (s35–s41). IMCAs can be involved in care reviews or adult protection; where adult protection is raised, an IMCA can be appointed even if there are family members (SCIE, 2021). IMCAs are a safeguard for people who lack capacity, ensuring they have support and representation with regard to decision making as well as making sure the MCA 2005 is being adhered to (SCIE, 2021). IMCAs will gather information; evaluate the information gathered, for example checking that the person who lacks capacity has been supported to be involved in the decision making; make representation and raise any concerns with the decision makers; and challenge decisions, for example if the IMCA has concerns and these are not resolved by consultation with the decision maker, the IMCA has the power to complain using local procedures or apply to the Court of Protection (SCIE, 2021).

SAFEGUARDING VULNERABLE ADULTS

Hardy (2017, p 1) highlights that the '*most difficult issue in adult social care, the one that puts the greatest test on social workers' professional judgement, is that of choice versus control, risk versus safety*' and that the MCA is vital as it provides a safeguard to balance autonomy and protection. The MCA 2005 protects the rights of vulnerable adults; for example, section 5 gives protection for people making a decision on someone's behalf in accordance with the MCA:

> *If a person does something in connection with the care or treatment of another person, they are protected if, before doing the act, they take reasonable steps to establish whether that person lacks capacity in relation to the matter in question, and, when doing the act, reasonably believe that the person lacks capacity in relation to the matter and it will be in the best interests for the act to be done.*
>
> (Brown et al, 2015, p7)

Also, people have to be deemed to have capacity (s1, Principle 1), rather than the other way round, meaning that regulated tests need to be conducted to ascertain if a person lacks capacity or not (s2, s3). Vulnerable people are additionally protected in terms of respecting their autonomy, so, for example, going back to the case study, Liliani may not be able to make a decision about going out in the middle of the night, but she can make decisions about what she wants to eat (s1, Principle 3).

An aspect that does need consideration with regard to safeguarding is section 1, Principle 2, which highlights that a person should not be treated as unable to make a decision unless all practical steps have been taken without success. So, when assessing an individual, consider if someone is drowsy at a certain time, for example as a result of medication. A time should be chosen when the person is not at their drowsiest, otherwise the assessment could be impaired and the person being assessed not safeguarded as they should be.

LASTING POWER OF ATTORNEY

A lasting power of attorney (LPA, s9) is a legal document that lets you (the 'donor') appoint one or more people (known as 'attorneys') to help you make decisions or to make decisions on your behalf. However, although most parts of the MCA 2005 apply to people 16 and over, some parts only apply to people 18 and over, for example making a lasting power of attorney.

The LPA (7.36 Mental Capacity Act 2005 Code of Practice, 2007) covers dealing with bank accounts and savings, claiming and using benefits, buying and/or selling property, dealing with shares and tax issues, paying bills, organising services such as day centre services and giving of presents or benevolences. Section 11 of the MCA 2005 also outlines that it could cover a person's welfare, including refusing or consenting to medical treatment; however, if the person's wishes are known before the person lacks capacity, the person's wishes, feelings and views should be adhered to.

To as far as possible protect the donor (the person appointing the attorney) from abuse, the formal requirements are set out in the Lasting Powers of Attorney, Enduring Powers of Attorney and Public Guardian Regulations (Mental Capacity Act 2005, Code of Practice 2007, No 1253; Brown et al, 2009). Attorneys that are appointed are bound by the requirement to act in the donor's best interests (s1, Principle 4), which is to assume capacity (s1, Principle 1) on the part of the donor (unless diagnosed otherwise, s2, s3), take all practical steps to help the person to make decisions (s1, Principle 2), as well as to include a duty of care in decision making, to carry out the donor's wishes and instruction and to act in good faith in the best interests of the donor (Brown et al, 2009).

DEPUTIES AND DECLARATIONS

The Court of Protection (s50) has the power to make declarations, such as make a decision (or decisions) on behalf of the person; or appoint a deputy (s19) to make decisions for someone who does not have capacity.

There are a number of forms to be completed. For example, to become and act as a deputy, there is the Court of Protection deputy form (COP1), an assessment of capacity form (COP3) and a deputy's declaration form (COP4). See www.gov.uk for further information.

ADVANCE DECISIONS

An advance decision (s24–s26) to refuse treatment lets your health care team know your wishes if you are not able to communicate them. If you decide to refuse life-sustaining treatment in the future, the advance decision needs to be completed well in advance, so for example, if a person were to suffer a stroke (Stroke Association, 2021) and had a do not resuscitate advance decision recorded, this could be given to the medical team and the person's advance wishes could be respected (see www.gov.uk for further details).

APPLICATIONS TO THE COURT OF PROTECTION AND PUBLIC GUARDIAN

In this section, we will be considering applications to the Court of Protection and the Public Guardian.

Court of Protection

If someone is found to lack capacity or is alleged to lack capacity, an application can be made to the Court of Protection (s50), which is a superior court that transpired as a result of the MCA 2005 (Mind, 2021).

There are several bodies and individuals who can apply to the Court of Protection, such as NHS Trusts, local authorities, an allegedly incapacitated person, or someone wanting to be able to deal with the money and property of a person lacking capacity (Mind, 2021). The Association of Directors of Adult Social Services (ADASS) and the Social Care Institute for Excellence (SCIE) published guidance for good practice when accessing the Court of Protection, outlining how to apply in terms of who has permission to apply, the application process, costs incurred in applying, and urgent and fast-track applications (SCIE, 2011).

Applications have to be made to the Court of Protection and are guided by strict regulations but the Court of Protection must always act in a person's best interests (Mind, 2021).

Public Guardian

The Office of the Public Guardian (OPG, s57–s60) in England and Wales was formed in 2007 and is a government body that, within the framework of the MCA 2005, monitors the activities of deputies (s19) and attorneys (s9, s11) who act to protect the affairs of people who lack the mental capacity for making decisions themselves. The public official known as the Public Guardian was established under s57 of the MCA and was appointed by the Lord Chancellor and Secretary of State for Justice. The Public Guardian is watched over by the Public Guardian Board, which was established under s59 of the MCA.

For more information, see the Office of the Public Guardian (2021).

DECISION, CHOICE AND EMPOWERMENT

It is important for students to understand the impact of their decision making on the public because social work is a people profession and, although social workers manage risk, they need to bear in mind *the law is applied only when needed*. Understanding the impact of decision making in the context of applying the law is important because in every decision you need the law to make the decisions but it needs to be person appropriate.

Although a person may be deemed to lack capacity (s2, s3) on some issues, for example where they live or whether they can manage their own finances, they may still be able to be autonomous in their choice of food, drink, clothing, television viewing, leisure choices, computer games etc (s1, Principle 3). It is important for social workers to understand the essentiality of empowerment and the role of social workers to support the people with whom they are working.

TRANSITIONING FROM CHILD TO ADULT SERVICES

Mencap is a charity for people with learning disabilities and campaigns for change to support people with learning difficulties to live healthy and happy lives. Mencap highlights that preparation for adulthood should happen from their earliest years and no later than by Year 9, when they are aged 13 or 14 (Mencap, 2021). Early preparation is important so that not only are the child/family/carers prepared, but also the local authority can make provision for services and support where needed because children who need social care support will need to transition to adult services and there should also be no gap in support (Council for Disabled Children, 2020; Mencap, 2021). Failure to prepare early could result in lack of services and support. Although the right to make a decision is set out in the MCA 2005, and if a child lacks capacity the decision must be in the child's best interests, the Council for Disabled Children (2015, p 4) highlight that with regard to decision making and the Children and Families Act 2014, *'[l]ocal authorities must ensure that children, their parents and young people are involved in discussions and decisions about their individual support and about local provision'*.

As already highlighted, the MCA applies to everyone aged 16+ except in certain circumstances, for example making a LPA, and explains what happens when a child is unable to make a specific decision for themselves. As with adults, the same principles of the MCA apply, for example the five principles (s1) and the two-stage test (s2, s3). Next, we are going to consider the case study of Lydia in the context of transitioning from child to adult services.

> ### *Case study*
>
> Lydia, aged 16, has mild–moderate learning difficulties as a result of foetal alcohol syndrome. Lydia's father died when Lydia was a year old and Lydia's mum still struggles with alcohol-related issues. Lydia has been receiving support from children's social care and is currently being assessed to see if she is eligible for adult services.

Under the MCA 2005 Lydia must be assumed to have capacity (s1, Principle 1), unless the two-stage test (s2, s3) confirms otherwise. As Lydia has a mild–moderate learning difficulty, information must be presented in appropriate formats, which may include photos, gestures, non-verbal communication or Makaton (supports the spoken word, accompanied by signs and symbols). It is also important that information relating to supporting Lydia's needs is gathered from a variety of sources, for example the family/ carer, specialist nurse, school and GP, to ensure as much information is collated as possible to ensure the best support is provided for her. When transitioning from child to adult services, each case is taken on an individual basis, so it is important that the MCA 2005 in conjunction with any other relevant legislation (Care Act 2014) is used wisely in order to provide children transitioning with the best possible service and support.

DUTIES AND RESPONSIBILITIES OF THE SOCIAL WORKER

Social workers work with the most vulnerable people in society and, as such, have a duty to not only work within the law (Mental Capacity Act 2005; Equality Act 2010; Care Act 2014) but also demonstrate best practice and work within Social Work England's professional standards which include the following.

1. Promoting the rights, strengths and well-being of people, families and communities.

2. Establishing and maintaining the trust of people.

3. Being accountable for the quality of their practice and the decision they make.

4. Maintaining their continuing professional development.

5. Acting safely, respectfully and with professional integrity.

6. Promoting ethical practice and reporting concerns.

(adapted from Social Work England, 2021)

A way of ensuring these standards are upheld is by understanding and applying social work law to practice and thus contributing to best practice. The MCA is important because, as highlighted earlier, a person's mental capacity could be affected at any stage in their life, and social workers need to understand the law to support the people with whom they are working.

A key aspect to consider conducive to a relationship-based approach to social work is *how you can maximise a person's ability and opportunity to make decisions*. Just because a person has been legally assessed as not having capacity, this should not prevent you from using your social work skills to try to work with them to support them to consider their options, understand their goals and understand the risks and opportunities they may face in the future.

THE MENTAL CAPACITY ACT – BRIEF SUMMARY

The Mental Capacity Act 2005 notes that people have the following rights.

○ A person will be assumed to have capacity (s1, Principle 1), unless when assessed under the two-stage test (s2, s3) they are deemed to lack capacity.

○ If a person lacks capacity all decisions should be made in the person's best interests (s1, Principle 4, s4).

○ If a person's liberty is taken away, then the least restrictive option (s1, Principle 5) must be applied.

○ A person may be able to be supported by an Independent Mental Capacity Advocate (IMCA, s35) who will listen to what the person wants and speak on their behalf, although the IMCA will not make decisions for a person.

○ The Court of Protection (s50) has the power to appoint a deputy (s19) to make decisions for someone who does not have capacity.

○ An advance decision (s24–s26) enables the person's wishes when they did have capacity to be communicated after they have lost capacity; and a lasting power of attorney (s9) enables a person to appoint one or more people to help make or make decisions on the person's behalf.

For more information see Mind (nd).

DECISIONS MADE ON CASE STUDIES

To enable you to see how the decisions were made, see below.

The case study relating to Liliani

Alexander tried to care for Liliani at home, but he could not manage her behaviour. Liliani was constantly trying to go out in the middle of the night and Alexander was exhausted and concerned for Liliani's safety. After an assessment, a psychiatric unit was considered unsuitable for Liliani's needs. However, a care home was deemed to be suitable, so Liliani was accommodated in a care home to ensure her safety; this was the least restrictive option (s1, Principle 5). However, at all times Liliani's best interests was considered (s1, Principle 4, s4).

The case study relating to Lydia

Lydia was assessed using the two-stage test (s2, s3) and assessed as not having capacity to make decisions about the care and support she would need when transitioning from child to adult services. Under the MCA 2005, Lydia's best interests were considered (s1, Principle 4, s4) and it was decided that as Lydia's mum could not provide the support she needed at this crucial time in her life, an IMCA would be appointed to support her and provide representation to enable Lydia to receive support and care services to meet her needs.

Key points to remember

Remember that everyone is an individual when applying the law. There may be two people who both have Alzheimer's disease/dementia or a learning difficulty but their condition will be unique to them; thus, applying legislation needs to be tailored to the individual, rather than being a case of one size fits all. The law is a tool to support and protect the people with whom you work and should be used appropriately; do not just explain the law, but apply it.

TEST YOUR LEGISLATIVE KNOWLEDGE

Answers are at the back of the book.

Questions

- How many parts are there to the Mental Capacity Act 2005 and what are they?

- What are the five principles of the Mental Capacity Act 2005? Name the section they come under.

- What is the two-stage test? What sections support it?

- How can you ensure you practise in a service user's best interest? What sections support this?

- What is the role of the Independent Mental Capacity Advocate (IMCA) and which section supports this role?

- What is the purpose of the Court of Protection? What section supports it?

CHAPTER SUMMARY

In summary, this chapter explored the Mental Capacity Act 2005 and its application to practice by considering the case studies of Liliani, Alexander and Lydia and applied legislation to them. Although these are case studies, the principles considered could apply in a practice situation out in the field.

Also considered were the three parts of the Act; Part 1 covers persons who lack capacity (s1–s62), Part 2 covers the Court of Protection and the Public Guardian (s45–63) and Part 3 was the miscellaneous and general part (s62–69).

We also outlined the five principles (s1), the importance of the least restrictive option (s1, Principle 5) and best interests (s1, Principle 4, s4); the two-stage test (s2, s3); the role of the IMCA (s35–s39); safeguarding adults (s5); LPA (s9, s11); deputies and declarations (s19); advance decisions (s24–s26); applications to the Court of Protection (s45–s63) and the Public Guardian (s57–s60).

The importance of understanding the impact of decision making was also considered because, as previously highlighted, it is essential to remember that social work is a people profession and although social workers manage risk, they need to bear in mind the law is applied only when needed, as well as when transitioning from child to adult services. Before considering the next chapter which focuses on Deprivation of Liberty Safeguards (DoLS), Liberty Protection Safeguards (LPS) and the Mental Capacity (Amendment) Act 2019, we would like to end this chapter by encouraging you to record your personal reflections and individual thoughts; you may like to write them directly into this book to keep for future reference.

END OF CHAPTER ACTIVITY TO CAPTURE PERSONAL REFLECTION AND INDIVIDUAL THOUGHTS

Critically reflect on this chapter and what you have learned, recording your own personal thoughts and feelings; use the mindmap to assist you. As with other chapters where you have been encouraged to record your reflections, again research which model of reflection you would like to use for this activity; perhaps for this exercise you might consider Kolb's (1984) reflective model, the experiential learning cycle where the person changes from being a participant in the experience to a reflector upon the experience (Brown and Rutter, 2008; Rutter and Brown, 2019), and then critically reflect in the context of the law; how could the MCA 2005 apply in practice? How would you have applied the MCA to the case studies of Liliani, Alexander and Lydia? Also consider if there are any anti-discriminatory practices or anti-oppressive practice issues (Equality Act 2010) that stand out for you.

The Mental Capacity (Amendment) Act 2019 Liberty Protection Safeguards (LPS) resulted from the Mental Capacity (Amendment) Act 2019 and will apply to care homes, nursing homes, hospitals, day services, supported living, sheltered housing and anyone aged 16 years or over, expected to come into force 2022

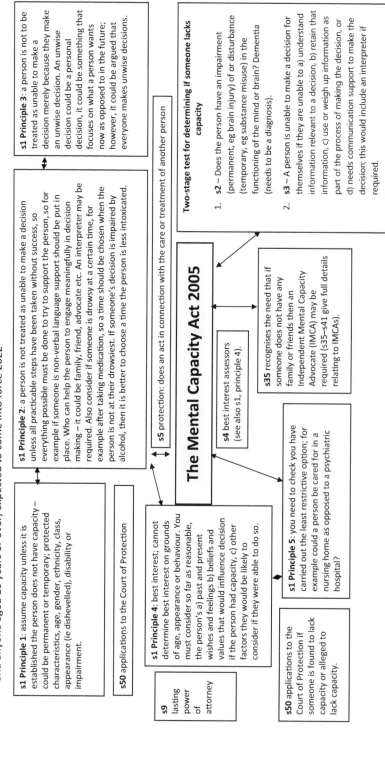

s1 Principle 1: assume capacity unless it is established the person does not have capacity – could be permanent or temporary; protected characteristics, age, gender, ethnicity, class, appearance (ie dishevelled), disability or impairment.

s50 applications to the Court of Protection

s9 lasting power of attorney

s1 Principle 4: best interest; cannot determine best interest on grounds of age, appearance or behaviour. You must consider so far as reasonable, the person's a) past and present wishes and feelings b) beliefs and values that would influence decision if the person had capacity, c) other factors they would be likely to consider if they were able to do so.

s50 applications to the Court of Protection if someone is found to lack capacity or alleged to lack capacity.

s1 Principle 5: you need to check you have carried out the least restrictive option; for example could a person be cared for in a nursing home as opposed to a psychiatric hospital?

s1 Principle 2: a person is not treated as unable to make a decision unless all practicable steps have been taken without success, so everything possible must be done to try to support the person, so for example if someone is non-verbal language support should be put in place. Who can help the person to engage meaningfully in decision making – it could be family, friend, advocate etc. An interpreter may be required. Also consider if someone is drowsy at a certain time, for example after taking medication, so a time should be chosen when the person is not at their drowsiest. If someone's decision is impaired by alcohol, then it is better to choose a time the person is less intoxicated.

The Mental Capacity Act 2005

s5 protection: does an act in connection with the care or treatment of another person

s4 best interest assessors (see also s1, principle 4).

s35 recognises the need that if someone does not have any family or friends then an Independent Mental Capacity Advocate (IMCA) may be required (s35–s41 give full details relating to IMCAs).

s1 Principle 3: a person is not to be treated as unable to make a decision merely because they make an unwise decision. An unwise decision could be a personal decision, it could be something that focuses on what a person wants now as opposed to in the future; however, it could be argued that everyone makes unwise decisions.

Two-stage test for determining if someone lacks capacity

1. **s2** – Does the person have an impairment (permanent, eg brain injury) of or disturbance (temporary, eg substance misuse) in the functioning of the mind or brain? Dementia (needs to be a diagnosis).

2. **s3** – A person is unable to make a decision for themselves if they are unable to a) understand information relevant to a decision, b) retain that information, c) use or weigh up information as part of the process of making the decision, or d) needs communication support to make the decision; this would include an interpreter if required.

Capture your personal reflection and individual thoughts here

REFERENCES

Alzheimer's Association (2020) Stages of Alzheimer's. [online] Available at: www.alz.org/alzheimers-dementia/stages (accessed 4 March 2022).

Brown, K and Rutter, L (2008) *Critical Thinking for Social Work*. London: Learning Matters Ltd/Sage.

Brown, R, Barber, P and Martin, D (2009) *The Mental Capacity Act 2005: A Guide for Practice*. 2nd ed. London: Learning Matters Ltd.

Brown, R, Barber, P and Martin, D (2015) *The Mental Capacity Act 2005: A Guide for Practice*. 3rd ed. London: Sage/Learning Matters.

Care Act 2014 [online] Available at: www.legislation.gov.uk/ukpga/2014/23/contents/enacted (accessed 4 March 2022).

Carr, H and Goosey, D (2017) *Law for Social Workers*. 14th ed. Oxford: Oxford University Press.

Council for Disabled Children (2015) *PfA Factsheet: The Mental Capacity Act 2005 and Supported Decision Making*. [online] Available at: www.preparingforadulthood.org.uk/SiteAssets/Downloads/pjlffgvj636383063305316403.pdf (accessed 4 March 2022).

Council for Disabled Children (2020) The Mental Capacity Act and Supported Decision Making. [online] Available at: https://councilfordisabledchildren.org.uk/resources/all-resources/filter/transition-adulthood/mental-capacity-act-2005-and-supported-decision (accessed 4 March 2022).

Dementia UK (2021) What is Dementia? [online] Available at: www.dementiauk.org/about-dementia/dementia-information/what-is-dementia (accessed 4 March 2022).

Equality Act 2010 [online] Available at: www.legislation.gov.uk/ukpga/2010/15/contents (accessed 4 March 2022).

Goldman, J S, Adamson, J, Karydas, A, Miller, B L and Hutton, M (2008) New Genes, New Dilemmas: FTLD Genetics and its Implications for Families. *American Journal of Alzheimer's Disease and Other Dementias*, 22(6): 507–15.

Griffiths, R (2012) What the 'Least Restrictive Option' Means Under the Mental Capacity Act. [online] Available at: www.communitycare.co.uk/2012/12/18/what-the-least-restrictive-option-means-under-the-mental-capacity-act (accessed 4 March 2022).

Hardy, R (2017) Safeguarding Adults Who Have Mental Capacity: Key Principles. [online] Available at: www.communitycare.co.uk/2017/12/04/safeguarding-adults-mental-capacity-key-principles (accessed 4 March 2022).

Human Rights Act 1998 [online] Available at: www.legislation.gov.uk/ukpga/1998/42/contents (accessed 4 March 2022).

Johns, R (2020) *Using the Law in Social Work*. London: Sage.

Kolb, D A (1984) *Experiential Learning: Experience as the Source of Learning and Development*. Englewood Cliffs, NJ: Prentice Hall.

Mencap (2021) Young People's Transition to Adulthood. [online] Available at: www.mencap.org.uk/advice-and-support/children-and-young-people/transition-adult-services (accessed 4 March 2022).

Mental Capacity Act (MCA) 2005 [online] Available at: www.legislation.gov.uk/ukpga/2005/9/contents (accessed 4 March 2022).

Mental Capacity Act (MCA) 2005 Explanatory Notes [online] Available at: www.legislation.gov.uk/ukpga/2005/9/notes/division/2? (accessed 4 March 2022).

Mental Capacity Act Code of Practice (2007) [online] Available at: https://assets.publishing.service.gov.uk/government/uploads/system/uploads/attachment_data/file/921428/Mental-capacity-act-code-of-practice.pdf (accessed 4 March 2022).

Mind (2021) The Court of Protection. [online] Available at: www.mind.org.uk/information-support/legal-rights/mental-capacity-act-2005/court-of-protection (accessed 4 March 2022).

Mind (nd) Quick Facts about the Mental Capacity Act 2005. [online] Available at: www.mind.org.uk/media-a/2908/mca-2005-2017.pdf (accessed 4 March 2022).

National Institute for Care and Excellence (NICE) (2021) Assessment of Capacity. [online] Available at: www.nice.org.uk/guidance/qs194/chapter/Quality-statement-3-Assessment-of-capacity (accessed 4 March 2022).

Office of the Public Guardian (2021) [online] Available at: www.gov.uk/government/organisations/office-of-the-public-guardian (accessed 4 March 2022).

Rutter, L and Brown, K (2019) *Critical Thinking and Professional Judgement for Social Work*. London: Sage.

Social Care Institute for Excellence (SCIE) (2011) Good Practice Guidance on Accessing the Court of Protection. [online] Available at: www.scie.org.uk/publications/guides/guide42 (accessed 4 March 2022).

Social Care Institute for Excellence (SCIE) (2014) *Best Interest Decision Making Checklist*. [online] Available at: www.scie.org.uk/files/mca/directory/best-interest-checklist.pdf?res=true (accessed 4 March 2022).

Social Care Institute for Excellence (SCIE) (2016) Mental Capacity Act 2005 at a Glance. [online] Available at: www.scie.org.uk/mca/introduction/mental-capacity-act-2005-at-a-glance#best-interests (accessed 4 March 2022).

Social Care Institute for Excellence (SCIE) (2021) What Do IMCAs Do and Who Should Get an IMCA? [online] Available at: www.scie.org.uk/mca/imca/do (accessed 4 March 2022).

Social Work England (2021) Professional Standards. [online] Available at: www.socialworkengland.org.uk/standards/professional-standards (accessed 4 March 2022).

Stroke Association UK (2021) What Is a Stroke? [online] Available at: www.stroke.org.uk/what-is-stroke (accessed 4 March 2022).

Deprivation of Liberty Safeguards and Liberty Protection Safeguards

INTRODUCTION

In this chapter we will examine Deprivation of Liberty Safeguards (DoLS) and Liberty Protection Safeguards (LPS) in the context of application to social work practice. This chapter will explore what DoLS and LPS are, why they were introduced, how Deprivation of Liberty is currently used and how LPS will be used in the future, and what their processes are. Additionally, understanding social workers' involvement will be deliberated.

DEPRIVATION OF LIBERTY SAFEGUARDS

What are Deprivation of Liberty Safeguards?

DoLS are used in a situation where a person's freedom is withdrawn in order to safeguard and protect them; so for example, if a person is diagnosed with Alzheimer's disease or dementia and deemed to lack capacity and accommodated in a care home or hospital setting and then the person tries to, or actually, leaves the care home/hospital, a DoLS would be applied for to protect them. Usually the care home or hospital would make the request for the DoLS process to be started and the assessment would be conducted by the local authority or the NHS body, respectively (Alzheimer's Society, 2021).

DoLS apply to all people aged 18 and over who are in a care home or hospital. The care home or hospital is called the managing authority.

DoLS were introduced by the Mental Health Act 2007 (s50) by adding a number of sections (fragments of a legal code to establish a requirement) and two new schedules (details attached to another document, eg an Act of Parliament) to the Mental Capacity Act 2005, which became known as the Deprivation of Liberty Safeguards or DoLS (Law Commission, 2017) and came into force in 2009 (NHS Digital, 2013).

Why were Deprivation of Liberty Safeguards introduced?

DoLS were introduced following findings from the European Court of Human Rights with regard to the case of *HL v UK 45508/99 [2004] ECHR 471I*, in which HL was deprived of his liberty (Clare et al, 2013; Parliament.UK, 2013a; SCIE, 2020c).

HL v UK 45508/99 [2004] ECHR 471I

HL was an adult male with autism and profound learning difficulties and had lived at Bournewood Hospital for 32 years prior to being cared for by Mr and Mrs E in their home for three years under a resettlement scheme (a Department of Health, Social Services and Public Safety 1995 initiative to move people living in hospitals to long-stay private homes to promote a better life). In 1997, HL became agitated following an incident at the day centre which he attended, and started banging his head on a wall and hitting himself on the head with his fists. HL was re-admitted back to Bournewood Hospital with clear direction that should HL try to leave Bournewood, he was to be sectioned under the Mental Health Act 1983. As HL never tried to leave the hospital, he was never sectioned and was an informal patient. However, during his stay at Bournewood, Mr and Mrs E, his carers, were not allowed to visit him as there were concerns from Bournewood that if he saw Mr and Mrs E, he may want to go home with them. Mr and Mrs E took the case to the court, positing that HL's rights had been breached under the European Convention of Human Rights. The European Court of Human Rights upheld the claim and directed that HL had been deprived of his liberty (Parliament.UK, 2013a).

How are Deprivation of Liberty Safeguards used?

DoLS are part of wider legislation and work in harmony with the Mental Capacity Act 2005 and Human Rights Act 1998 to protect the rights of people who are deemed to lack capacity (Age UK, 2022). The Social Care Institute for Excellence highlights that:

> There are estimated to be some 2 million people in England and Wales at any one time who are unable to consent, in whole or part, to their care and treatment. In 2015–16, 195,840 deprivations of liberty applications were made, and a little over 105,000 assessments were completed. In 76,530 (73 per cent) of these, the deprivation was authorised. Of the applications, 35,635 came from acute and mental health hospitals in the public and independent sectors. These figures compare with the roughly 11,000 applications made annually in hospitals and care homes combined prior to the 2014 Supreme Court judgement.
>
> (SCIE, 2021, p 1)

Although the intentions of DoLS are to protect an individual, abuse still takes place, for example in the case of Winterbourne View.

Winterbourne View

A serious case review was commissioned by South Gloucestershire Multi-Agency Safeguarding Adult Board, and prepared by independent adult safeguarding expert Margaret Flynn, to investigate practices at a private hospital called Winterbourne View following a BBC *Panorama* programme that aired in May 2011 showing people with learning difficulties suffering terrible abuse at the hands of staff at the hospital. Following the review '*11 members of staff were sentenced for criminal acts*' (Flynn, 2012, p 8).

Once this level of abuse was exposed in one hospital, the Care Quality Commission (CQC) were then commissioned to '*review 150 hospitals and care homes that provided care for people with learning difficulties*' (Parliament.UK, 2013b, p 6). The Winterbourne View case highlighted that human rights were not recognised and people were abused (Human Rights Act 1998; Equality Act 2010; Mencap, 2021). In this case, DoLS did not protect vulnerable adults, highlighting that the law can only be used in a person's best interests when the law is integrated into practice. However, where DoLS are applied for, it shows that the managerial team and staff caring for vulnerable people understand that the people in their care have the rights to be protected and treated with dignity and respect, while at all times promoting the person's best interests even if an individual is not in a position to make their own decisions (Flynn, 2012).

As in earlier chapters, a case study will be applied in the context of DoLS.

Case study

Wunmi is 85 years of age and lives independently in her own home until one day she suffers a stroke while out shopping. An ambulance is called and Wunmi is taken to hospital. Wunmi's two sons, Benjamin and Emmanuel, are contacted and they immediately go to the hospital.

Wunmi's mental capacity has been affected by the stroke and she is now an in-patient in hospital. Wunmi is constantly trying to leave the hospital in the middle of the night and is at risk of falls and thus needs protecting and safeguarding. The hospital advise Benjamin and Emmanuel that they are going to conduct a mental capacity assessment, which finds Wunmi is deemed to lack capacity. The next step is for the hospital to apply for a DoLS; again, Benjamin and Emmanuel are advised. Initially, Wunmi's two sons are shocked, upset and overwhelmed as prior to her stroke their mum was in fairly good health for her age, had a great sense of humour and was independent – depriving her of her liberty sounds harsh and unreasonable.

What is the Deprivation of Liberty Safeguards process?

Guidance about how to put DoLS into practice has been provided by the Social Care Institute for Excellence (SCIE, 2017), which is an independent charity working with health care, housing and adults', families' and children's care and support services across the United Kingdom.

DoLS are conducted by trained professionals called best interests assessors (BIAs), which could be a social worker, an Approved Mental Health Professional (AMHP), nurse, occupational therapist or chartered psychologist, and the mental health assessor, who is a medical doctor, usually a psychiatrist, who assesses if a person who is likely to have their liberty deprived has a mental health issue. The BIA is usually the main assessor and the mental health assessor may also assess for capacity. Anyone can request a DoLS assessment; however, it is usually the care provider, eg the care home or hospital, that will request DoLS (Alzheimer's Society, 2021). The assessment involves age, mental health, mental capacity, best interests, eligibility and no refusals (Alzheimer's Society, 2021).

SCIE (2017) provided guidance for applying DoLS and highlighted the importance of staff training to ensure that staff understand what it means to put a safeguard in place and how to assess to see if a person's liberty is deprived in order to safeguard them and others. SCIE also outlined that there should also be organisational policies and procedures with clear guidelines relating to levels of responsibility and situations in which DoLS can be used. In addition, there should be guidance on care planning which highlights that, where possible, alternatives should be sought to prevent deprivation of liberty and that good and effective care planning in accordance with the Mental Capacity Act 2005 is essential and has to be in the best interests of the person. Additionally, arrangements for training on restriction and restraint should be made because staff need to be aware that if movement is restricted, this could be depriving a person of their liberty. Procedures for scrutinising care plans so that hospitals adhere to selecting the least restrictive option to prevent harm while at the same time safeguarding the individual are also required (SCIE, 2017). Family/carers and significant others where possible should also be consulted to ascertain as much information about the individual as possible; if this is not possible, an Independent Mental Capacity Advocate (IMCA, see Chapter 6), may be appropriate (SCIE, 2017, 2020b).

SCIE (2017) further outline that an audit including clear and accurate records should be kept with DoLS applications to safeguard delivery, with records of senior staff that are authorised to sign off applications so that if there is a CQC inspection or any other body requires access to records there is transparency. As the process needs to be transparent, there should also be a named person who has the duty to report DoLS applications and outcomes to the hospital board supervising quality as well as the CQC and who also has responsibility to respond to CQC reports with regard to the hospital's compliance with the Mental Capacity Act 2005 and DoLS (SCIE, 2017).

SCIE highlight there should also be a policy on working in partnership with supervisory bodies (usually the local authorities), which includes supporting BIAs (DoLS regulation 66) who are responsible for '*deciding whether a restrictive situation is authorised by Sections 5 and 6 of the MCA or whether it amounts to a deprivation of the person's liberty'* (SCIE, 2020a, p 1). If after considering the evidence collated, the BIA determines that the person is deprived of their liberty, they are then required to *'holistically assess'* if the restrictions are in an individual's best interests and if they are *'proportionate to the risk and seriousness of harm to that person without the proposed restriction'* (SCIE, 2020a, p 1). The policy should also include supporting BIAs who could be a qualified social worker, nurse, occupational therapist or psychologist. So if the BIA was a social worker, they must not be involved in the person's current care and support or in a position where they make decisions for their care, but they are there to gain information from family/carers and significant others. However, should a situation arise where a BIA (Mental Capacity Act 2005, s4) finds that, although an individual has been deprived of their liberty, it is not in their best interests then there should be arrangements for an urgent review of the care plan (SCIE, 2017); this would also require a policy on who has responsibility for preparing the review of care plans. Finally, there should be a policy relating to reviewing authorisations and actions that should be taken if and when a deprivation of liberty authorisation finishes (SCIE, 2017).

DoLS application forms are usually electronic and stored at the hospital or care home; however, to find out how to access them, the supervisory body (usually the local authority) should be the first point of contact. Having considered the DoLS process, next social workers' involvement will be explored.

How are social workers involved?

As previously highlighted, DoLS are conducted by trained professionals called BIAs (Hubbard, 2018), which could be a qualified social worker together with the mental health assessor. The social worker's responsibility as a BIA is to promote well-being and protect vulnerable people (Human Rights Act 1998). If the social worker is a BIA, they become involved when the referral has been made to the local authority or NHS body. The social worker's role is to make decisions in the best interests of the individual in accordance with the BIA guidance, as considered above.

Returning to the case study of Wunmi, the social worker supporting her would need to not only carry out her duty to safeguard Wunmi to keep her safe but also, as highlighted in number one of Social Work England's professional standards, promote the rights, strengths and well-being of the family (Social Work England, 2021). Being able to explain DoLS in a succinct and easy-to-understand way will enable the social worker to not only protect the vulnerable people with whom they are working, but also convey the intricacies of DoLS to families in an empathic, sensitive manner and promote their well-being as well as safeguard the service user.

Although social workers are currently working within the DoLS framework, DoLS are to be replaced by Liberty Protection Safeguards (LPS) in the future; therefore, these will be explored next.

LIBERTY PROTECTION SAFEGUARDS – MENTAL CAPACITY (AMENDMENT) ACT 2019

What are Liberty Protection Safeguards?

LPS follow the same principle as DoLS and are where a person's freedom or liberty is withdrawn in order to safeguard and protect them. LPS arose as a result of the 2019 amendments to the Mental Capacity Act 2005. They are new standards which are due to be implemented in 2022 and expected to run alongside DoLS for approximately a year (however, in some cases it is anticipated that DoLS will remain until they expire) to contribute towards ease of transitioning. In the meantime, understanding the principles of DoLS is useful to form an understanding about how and when liberty is affected. Although the target date for implementation of the LPS was originally 2020, implementation was delayed; thus, until LPS are implemented, the MCA Code of Practice (2013) provides guidance (Law Commission, 2017).

LPS will apply to individuals aged 16 or over who need to be safeguarded by being deprived of their liberty and who reside in care homes, nursing homes, hospitals, day services, supported living, the person's own home, a family home, shared lives (individual with difficulties is matched with a host family to live with them as part of the family while also receiving support), supported living (scheme to assist people with difficulties to live as independent lives as possible) or sheltered housing (housing for disabled or vulnerable people with support from a scheme manager) without the need to go to court (Department of Health and Social Care, 2021). As there is no formal definition for deprivation of liberty, the acid test (SCIE, 2021), as set out by Lady Hale (Supreme Court) following a review of the Cheshire West case, outlines that a person is deprived of their liberty if 1) they are subject to continuous supervision and control and 2) are not free to leave.

Why were Liberty Protection Safeguards introduced?

LPS were introduced to reform elements of DoLS; for example, DoLS currently only apply to care home and hospital settings and are not transferable, while under the terms of LPS, safeguards apply to not only care homes, nursing homes and hospitals, but also domestic settings as indicated earlier such as day services, supported living, sheltered housing, and so on. Additionally, whereas DoLS applied to people aged 18 and over, LPS will apply to people 16 and over. Finally, whereas DoLS could be applied when people have already been deprived of their liberty, LPS have to be authorised in advance by the responsible body (usually the local authority, clinical commissioning body or NHS body) which replaces the current supervisory board before a person can be deprived of their liberty. To illustrate how LPS can safeguard individuals, next the Cheshire West case will be deliberated to demonstrate issues that can arise without appropriate safeguards in place.

Cheshire West case

The Cheshire West case involved three individuals including two sisters who had learning difficulties, lacked capacity and had additional needs and who were under continuous supervision and not allowed to leave their residence (Law Commission, 2017; Rebours, 2017). The Supreme Court was asked to consider the case and see whether these three individuals were being deprived of their liberty without relevant safeguard protections in place.

Initially the court ruled that as continuous supervision would not be unusual for any individual with a high number of needs, and all three individuals were well cared for, then liberty was not deprived (Rebours, 2017). However, a ruling five years later determined that even if a person does not have capacity and does not express a desire to leave their residence, if they are being prevented from leaving, it still remained the case that the three individuals were being deprived of their liberty (Rebours, 2017). Lady Hale said in the Supreme Court:

> The fact that my living arrangements are comfortable, and indeed make my life as enjoyable as it could possibly be, should make no difference. A gilded cage is still a cage.

> (Rebours, 2017, p 2)

How will Liberty Protection Safeguards be used?

LPS will be used to protect people who are already, or who need to be, deprived of their liberty to facilitate their care or treatment and who lack mental capacity to make their own decisions or consent to their arrangements (Department of Health and Social Care, 2021). Individuals who may have an LPS authorisation could include people with Alzheimer's disease, dementia, autism or learning difficulties or who have had a stroke.

The responsible body will provide approval for care, support or treatment under the LPS. If an application and approval for an LPS is needed, the responsible body needs to be notified in order to begin the LPS process. Anyone can make a referral and this could be via email or using the official forms (Department of Health and Social Care, 2015; SCIE, 2017).

What is the Liberty Protection Safeguards process?

The LPS comprises three assessments:

○ capacity assessment (to assess capacity to make decisions);

○ medical assessment (to determine if a person has a mental disorder);

○   a necessary and proportionate assessment (to determine if the arrangements are necessary to prevent harm to the person and proportionate to the likelihood and seriousness of that harm).

(Department of Health and Social Care, 2021)

Existing assessments and care planning (for example, under the Care Act 2014) will be used if it reasonable and appropriate (Department of Health and Social Care, 2021).

In certain circumstances, the responsible body may ask the care home manager to organise the assessment. The LPS also replaces BIAs, introducing the new role of Approved Mental Capacity Professional (AMCP) to deal with more complex cases, as well as expanding the role of the Independent Mental Capacity Advocate (IMCA, Mental Capacity Act 2005, s35), a person who is an *advocate instructed under the Mental Capacity Act 2005 who is responsible for supporting and representing a person who lacks capacity to make certain decisions* (Law Commission, 2017, p 3). It is important for social workers to know about LPS as these will be coming into effect in the future; understanding the LPS framework now will enable them to be prepared and able to support the people with whom they will be working when LPS are implemented.

The reason for including LPS in this chapter is the same as for DoLS, because social workers work with the most vulnerable people in society and need to be prepared mentally and emotionally to work with people in the most difficult times in their lives. However, social workers also need to recognise the impact these complex situations may have on their own mental health and well-being. Being confident to work with service users in an assertive but sensitive manner is a skill which can be enhanced by understanding legislative frameworks applicable to social work practice. Having considered how deprivation of liberty affects adults, next depriving children of liberty will be briefly considered.

DEPRIVING CHILDREN OF THEIR LIBERTY

As mentioned earlier, for a deprivation of liberty to be authorised under DoLS a person has to be 18 years of age, although an assessment can be conducted when a young person is 17 years of age provided they are 18 years of age *by the time the authorisation takes effect* (Brown et al, 2009, p 100). However, as considered earlier, once LPS is introduced the age for deprivation of liberty will be 16 years.

While often parents/carers will make decisions for a child or young person under 18 years (Wheeler, 2013), other legislation such as the Children Act 1989 (s47, see Chapter 3), Mental Health Act 1983 (s63, see Chapter 8) and the Mental Capacity Act 2005 (young people over the age of 16 years, see Chapter 6) enables children to be deprived of their liberty to prevent significant harm (Children Act 1989, s47), be restrained or be detained. If a child lacks capacity and needs to be detained, the Court of Protection needs to authorise it (Wheeler, 2013). The Court of Protection can also authorise detention of a child who has capacity, if they are not detained under the Mental Health Act 1983 (Wheeler, 2013).

A child can also be deprived of their liberty if they are looked after or cared for away from home (Children Act 1989, s31, s38 or s20 pending legal proceedings, see Chapter 4), looked after in secure accommodation (Children Act 1989, s25), subject to sectioning under the Mental Health Act 1983 or subject to sentencing through the Powers of Criminal Courts (Sentencing) Act 2000 (Chapter 5), although children are protected under Article 5 of the European Convention of Human Rights not to be deprived of their liberty without legal authorisation.

When a 16 or 17 year-old needs to be deprived of their liberty under DoLS, an application must be made to the Court of Protection; however, as identified earlier, under the LPS, responsible bodies (local authorities and NHS bodies) are able to authorise the arrangements without a court order (Department of Health and Social Care, 2021).

While this area of social work practice has been briefly discussed in this chapter, as highlighted in this section, other chapters (3, 4, 5) in the book discuss children being deprived of liberty in more detail.

What is the social worker's involvement?

Social workers may be working in vulnerable children or adult settings and thus need to understand which legislation can be used to support the people with whom they are working. For example, they need to know when to apply legislation such as the Children Act 1989, Mental Health Act 1983 and Mental Capacity Act 2005 (young people aged 16–17 years) or how DoLS and LPS work in practice when working with adults and young people. As highlighted in Chapter 6, life is unpredictable and a person never knows when they may be in a position where they are subject to a DoLS authorisation and social work support may be needed. Social workers need to practise in harmony with other legislation such as the Mental Capacity Act 2005 (Chapter 6) and the Care Act 2014 (Chapter 10) to ensure best practice in the best interests of the person with whom they are working in partnership.

Depriving a person of their liberty is a complex and challenging area of legislative framework since depriving someone of their liberty, even if it is in their best interests and safeguards them, should not be taken lightly (SCIE, 2017). Social workers need to be aware that not only are there impacts on the person who is being deprived of their liberty, but it can also be an extremely emotional time for family/carers and significant others, as we learned in the case study of Wunmi and the effect on her sons Benjamin and Emmanuel. Deprivation of liberty may have occurred due to a sudden event such as stroke, as highlighted in the case study of Wunmi, accident or trauma; therefore, one minute the family/carers' loved one may have been healthy and well and the next the person is debilitated. Often when a loved one is deprived of their liberty, family/carers and significant others will not understand why it is necessary or what the process is, feel shock at the fact the suggestion is being made, feel heartache that it is necessary and worry about how the person will be restrained should a situation arise where deprivation of liberty has to be enforced. Social workers have a key role in helping family/carers and significant others understand that it is for the individual's protection, and that all other less restrictive options and possibilities would have been explored before a deprivation of liberty application is made.

The social worker also needs to understand whom safeguards apply to, who is responsible for applying safeguards, when an application should be considered, what the timescales are for assessments, what happens if authorisation is granted and what happens when it is refused (SCIE, 2017).

DoLS – brief summary

- The Mental Capacity Act Deprivation of Liberty Safeguards (MCA DoLS) were introduced by the Mental Health Act 2007 and came into effect in 2009.

- DoLS applies to people aged 18 and over.

- DoLS was introduced following findings from the European Court of Human Rights with regard to the case of *HL v UK 45508/99 [2004] ECHR 471I*, in which HL was deprived of his liberty.

- DoLS does not apply to children under 18, although an assessment can be made when a young person is 17 years of age provided they are 18 years old by the time the authorisation comes into effect.

- The Winterbourne View case highlighted DoLS were not used, human rights were not recognised and people were abused; thus safeguards such as DoLS to protect and safeguard people are essential.

LPS – brief summary

- The 2019 amendments to the Mental Capacity Act 2005 resulted in LPS, which are due to come into effect in 2022.

- LPS apply to people aged 16 and over.

- LPS will apply to care homes, nursing homes, hospitals, day services, supported living, shared lives, sheltered housing, and own/family homes.

- AMCP will replace BIA.

Decisions made on case study

Wunmi's mental capacity was affected by a stroke, which resulted in her being hospitalised. After she attempted to leave the hospital, the decision to apply for a DoLS was made to safeguard her.

Key points to remember

Remember that DoLS and LPS are frameworks to ensure best interests, protection and safeguarding of individuals if they are deemed to lack capacity, and are essential to contribute to good social work practice. As we learned from Bournewood Hospital and Winterbourne View, even though frameworks are put into place to protect vulnerable people who lack capacity, these can be susceptible to abuse. As social workers you need to understand DoLS and LPS and how to apply them in practice to safeguard and protect the people with whom you are working.

TEST YOUR LEGISLATIVE KNOWLEDGE

Answers are at the back of the book.

Questions

Deprivation of Liberty Safeguards

- What was the result of the 2009 amendment to the MCA 2005?

- What age does DoLS begin to apply?

- How did the case of *HL v UK 45508/99 [2004] ECHR 471I* impact the law?

- Why is the Winterbourne View serious case review important?

Liberty Protection Standards

- What was the result of the 2019 amendment?

- At what age do LPS begin to apply?

- To whom will LPS apply when they come into effect?

- What is the name of the replacement BIA role?

CHAPTER SUMMARY

In summary, this chapter has explored DoLS, which apply to all people aged 18 and over and were introduced in 2009 following findings from the European Court of Human Rights with regard to the case of *HL v UK 45508/99 [2004] ECHR 471I*. DoLS have been deliberated in the context of the case study relating to Wunmi, and as previously stated, although this is a case study, principles apply in practice. Also discussed was the Winterbourne View case in which a serious case review took place investigating practices which showed people with learning difficulties suffering terrible abuse at the hands of the staff at the hospital, thus identifying that safeguards such as DoLS are imperative to protect vulnerable people.

Furthermore, LPS, which came about as a result of the 2019 amendment to the Mental Capacity Act 2005 and are expected to come into effect in 2022, were also discussed. LPS apply to all people aged 16 and over in care homes, nursing homes, hospitals, day services, supported living, sheltered housing and own/family homes. The next chapter will explore the Mental Health Act 1983/2007.

END OF CHAPTER ACTIVITY TO CAPTURE PERSONAL REFLECTIONS AND INDIVIDUAL THOUGHTS

Critically reflect on this chapter and what you have learned, recording your own personal thoughts and feelings. The reflective model you might like to reflect upon in this chapter is Maclean's (2016) model for social work reflection, 'whatever the weather', which uses the weather to critically reflect upon different elements of social work practice. For example, sunshine reflects what went well; rain, what did not go so well; fog, did you get lost and not know what to do; thunder, where there is so much going on it is difficult to think; snow, was there something you saw differently today; lightning, did something surprise you; wind, were you blown off course; and storm, conflicts arising. Also, as in previous chapters, consider if there are any anti-discriminatory or anti-oppressive practice issues (Equality Act 2010) that stand out for you.

Capture your personal reflections and individual thoughts here

REFERENCES

Age UK (2022) Deprivation of Liberty Safeguards. [online] Available at: www.ageuk.org.
uk/globalassets/age-uk/documents/factsheets/fs62deprivation%20of%20liberty_
safeguards_fcs.pdf (accessed 25 April 2022).

Alzheimer's Society (2021) Deprivation of Liberty Safeguards. [online] Available at: www.
alzheimers.org.uk/get-support/legal-financial/deprivation-liberty-safeguards-dols-
assessment (accessed 4 March 2022).

Brown, R, Barber, P and Martin, D (2009) *The Mental Capacity Act 2005: A Guide for
Practice*. 2nd ed. London. Learning Matters Ltd.

Care Act 2014 [online] Available at: www.legislation.gov.uk/ukpga/2014/23/contents
(accessed 4 March 2022).

Children Act 1989 [online] Available at: www.legislation.gov.uk/ukpga/1989/41/contents
(accessed 4 March 2022).

Clare, I C H, Redley, M, Keeling, A, Wagner, A P, Wheeler, J R, Gunn, M J and Holland, A J
(2013) *Understanding the Interface between the Mental Capacity Act's
Deprivation of Liberty Safeguards (MCA-DoLS) and the Mental Health Act (MHA)*.
Cambridge: Cambridge Intellectual & Developmental Disabilities Research Group,
Department of Psychiatry, University of Cambridge.

Department of Health and Social Care (2015) Deprivation of Liberty Safeguard: Resources.
[online] Available at: www.gov.uk/government/publications/deprivation-of-liberty-
safeguards-forms-and-guidance (accessed 4 March 2022).

Department of Health and Social Care (2021) Liberty Protection Safeguards: What They Are.
[online] Available at: www.gov.uk/government/publications/liberty-protection-safeguards-
factsheets/liberty-protection-safeguards-what-they-are (accessed 4 March 2022).

Equality Act 2010 [online] Available at: www.legislation.gov.uk/ukpga/2010/15/contents
(accessed 4 March 2022).

Flynn, M (2012) Serious Case Review (Winterbourne View). [online] Available at: www.
southglos.gov.uk/news/serious-case-review-winterbourne-view (accessed 4
March 2022).

Hubbard, R (2018) Best Interests Assessor Role: An Opportunity or a 'Dead End' for Adult
Social Workers? *Practice: Social Work in Action*, 30(2): 83–98.

Human Rights Act 1998 [online] Available at: www.legislation.gov.uk/ukpga/1998/42/
contents (accessed 4 March 2022).

Law Commission (2017) *Mental Capacity and Deprivation of Liberty*. Report. [online]
Available at: www.lawcom.gov.uk/project/mental-capacity-and-deprivation-of-liberty
(accessed 7 March 2022).

Maclean, S (2016) A New Model for Social Work Reflection: Whatever the Weather.
Professional Social Work, March: 28–29.

Mencap (2021) 10 Years since Winterbourne. [online] Available at: www.mencap.org.uk/get-involved/campaign-mencap/governments-broken-promise-transform-care (accessed 4 March 2022).

Mental Capacity Act 2005 [online] Available at: www.legislation.gov.uk/ukpga/2005/9/contents (accessed 4 March 2022).

Mental Capacity Act Code of Practice (2007) [online] Available at: https://assets.publishing.service.gov.uk/government/uploads/system/uploads/attachment_data/file/921428/Mental-capacity-act-code-of-practice.pdf (accessed 4 March 2022).

Mental Health Act 1983 [online] Available at: www.legislation.gov.uk/ukpga/1983/20/contents (accessed 15 December 2021.

Mental Health Act 2007 [online] Available at: www.legislation.gov.uk/ukpga/2007/12/contents (accessed 14 December 2021).

NHS Digital (2013) Mental Capacity Act 2005, Deprivation of Liberty Safeguards Assessments, England 2012–13. Annual Report. [online] Available at: https://digital.nhs.uk/data-and-information/publications/statistical/mental-capacity-act-2005-deprivation-of-liberty-safeguards-assessments/mental-capacity-act-2005-deprivation-of-liberty-safeguards-assessments-england-2012-13-annual-report (accessed 29 March 2022).

Parliament.UK (2013a) *Mental Capacity Act 2005: Post-legislative Scrutiny – Select Committee on the Mental Capacity Act 2005: Deprivation of Liberty Safeguards.* [online] Available at: https://publications.parliament.uk/pa/ld201314/ldselect/ldmentalcap/139/13911.htm (accessed 4 March 2022).

Parliament.UK (2013b) *Transforming Care: A National Response to Winterbourne View Hospital. Department of Health Review: Final Report.* [online] Available at: https://publications.parliament.uk/pa/ld201314/ldselect/ldmentalcap/139/13911.htm (accessed 4 March 2022).

Powers of Criminal Courts (Sentencing) Act 2000 [online] Available at: www.legislation.gov.uk/ukpga/2000/6/contents (accessed 8 March 2022).

Rebours, J (2017) The Cheshire West Case: Three Years on and the Right Liberty. [online] Available at: www.bihr.org.uk/blog/cheshirewest2017 (accessed 4 March 2022).

Social Care Institute for Excellence (SCIE) (2017) *Deprivation of Liberty Safeguards: Putting Them into Practice.* [online] Available at: www.scie.org.uk/files/mca/dols/practice/putting-dols-into-practice.pdf (accessed 4 March 2022).

Social Care Institute for Excellence (SCIE) (2020a) DoLS Best Interests Assessment. [online] Available at: www.scie.org.uk/mca/dols/practice/assessments/best-interests (accessed 4 March 2022).

Social Care Institute for Excellence (SCIE) (2020b) IMCA: Applications for Further DoLS Authorisations. [online] Available at: www.scie.org.uk/mca/imca/roles/further-dols-authorisations (accessed 4 March 2022).

Social Care Institute for Excellence (SCIE) (2020c) Use of DoLs in Hospitals – Bournewood. [online] Available at: www.scie.org.uk/mca/dols/practice/hospital#bournewood (accessed 4 March 2022).

Social Care Institute for Excellence (SCIE) (2021) Liberty Protection Safeguards. [online] Available at: www.scie.org.uk/mca/lps/latest (accessed 4 March 2022).

Social Work England (2021) Professional Standards. [online] Available at: www. socialworkengland.org.uk/standards/professional-standards (accessed 4 March 2022).

Wheeler, R (2013) The Mental Capacity Act 2005 Makes (Temporary) Restriction of Liberty Lawful. *Archives of Disease in Childhood-Education and Practice*, 98 (2): 80.

The Mental Health Act 1983/2007

INTRODUCTION

This chapter considers the Mental Health Act 1983 and the 2007 amendment to the Act. The main purpose of the Mental Health Act (MHA) 1983/2007 is to assess, treat and uphold the rights of people who experience mental health issues when they are at risk of harm to themselves or other people and may be sectioned (s2, s3). This chapter is important because people experiencing mental health issues have the potential to arise in various areas of social work practice, not just if you are a social worker working in mental health services. For example, a person with Usher syndrome who is receiving sensory (Deaf/deafblind and visual) services may experience depression or suicidal thoughts and feelings, so although their primary support is provided through a sensory service, they may need mental health support too. This chapter is important to social work practice because, as highlighted by Mind (2020a), one in four people in the United Kingdom will experience a mental health problem each year. Additionally, during the Covid-19 pandemic, concern for people's mental health has risen, due to individuals worrying about the effect Covid-19 will have on their lives and worrying about their future (Marshal et al, 2020).

Although there have been plans to reform mental health services, '*the government has not been able to bring forward this White Paper as early as originally planned – because of the unprecedented battle we are waging with the COVID-19 pandemic*' (Department of Health and Social Care, 2021, p 1). However, there are plans for review and under the review, one of the aims is to improve mental health services for people of Black, Asian and minority ethnic backgrounds and the '*government asked the Independent Review to take a close look at the disparities that exist and to make proposals to address them*' (Department of Health and Social Care, 2021, p 1). The report also highlighted that they '*have seen high profile cases of quality failings in the care of people with a learning disability and autistic people in in-patient settings such as the abuse uncovered at Whorlton Hall in May 2019*' (Department of Health and Social Care, 2021, p 2).

Whorlton Hall

Whorlton Hall was an assessment and treatment unit for people who experienced learning disabilities, autism or complex needs, for example, challenging behaviour. An undercover reporter recorded clips showing '*staff deliberately taunting, threatening, and provoking people detained in the unit under the Mental Health Act. People were shown in extreme distress after deliberate exposure to completely avoidable triggers*' (Murphy, 2019, p 1).

The Whorlton Hall case resonates with what happened at Winterbourne View (see Chapter 7) and highlights the need for ongoing improvement in services ensconced in legislative frameworks to support vulnerable people. The legislation in place to support and protect people with mental health issues is the MHA 1983/2007; however, the NHS have a long-term mental health implementation plan (*NHS Mental Health Implementation Plan 2019/20–2023/24*) which provides a new framework to ensure the NHS deliver on their commitment to improve mental health services (NHS, 2019a). The summary of the Five Year Forward View for Mental Health and Long-Term Plan commitments highlights that:

> *The NHS Long Term Plan (LTP) makes a renewed commitment that mental health services will grow faster than the overall NHS budget with a ringfenced investment worth at least £2.3 billion a year for mental health services by 2023/24. Children and young people's mental health services will grow faster than both overall NHS funding and total mental health spending. By 2020/21, all Five Year Forward View for Mental Health (FYFVMH) ambitions will be met, forming the basis of further growth and transformation.*

> (NHS, 2019a, p 5)

Development of mental health services is important for social work practice because health inequalities and variations in care can result in the life expectancy of people with severe mental health issues being '*up to 20 years less than the general population*' (NHS, 2019c, p 7).

Although it is positive news that the government plan to review mental health services, until changes are implemented the legislation social workers work with is the Mental Health Act 1983/2007, with some changes being made to section 135 and section 136 with regard to police holding powers. As the Mental Health Act cannot be covered in its entirety, this chapter will introduce you to the ten parts of the Act as well as demonstrating how the MHA applies in practice using a case study approach: a case study of Ava for adults and a case study of B for children.

Case study

Ava is 29 years of age; she moved from a small village in the north of England where she lived with her mother to a big city nearer to the south of England to start a new job. Ava missed her mother, found it difficult to make friends and experienced loneliness and isolation. Ava was working for a small company as an administrator and although she had experienced mild depression most of her life, one day she confided in a colleague that she was hearing voices and got very angry and abusive when the colleague said she could not hear the voices; Ava's behaviour became so uncontrollable that the police were called. When the police arrived, Ava threatened suicide saying that the police were aliens that had come to kidnap her and take her to another planet. Ava was taken to hospital where she was diagnosed with schizophrenia.

SECTIONS OF THE MENTAL HEALTH ACT 1983

In most cases, people with mental health issues are treated with their consent in hospitals or other mental health facilities and their admission is informal (MHA 1983, s131), but in some cases people are detained (MHA 1983, s2, s3, s4, s37), which is also referred to as sectioning, and treated without their consent (NHS, 2019b). If someone is at risk to themselves or others, the main piece of legislation used to section someone is the MHA 1983 (NHS, 2019b). Returning to the case study, in this instance the police and the Approved Mental Health Professional (AMHP, who can co-ordinate your assessment and admission to hospital) calmed the situation by contacting Ava's mum via video conferencing and Ava was informally admitted to hospital under section 131, which was the least restrictive option (Thomas et al, 2015) and prevented compulsory detention (s2, s3).

As indicated earlier, the MHA 1983 is a complex and intricate piece of legislation and as such it would not be possible for you to memorise it all; that is why it is important to conduct personal research, and liaise with experts of experience and experts in the field. The Act is divided into ten parts and a brief overview is given below.

- Part 1: Application of the Act (s1).

- Part 2: Compulsory admission to hospital and guardianship, including procedures for hospital admission (s2–s6); guardianship (s7–s10); general provisions as to applications and recommendations (s11–s15); position of patient subject to detention or guardianship (s16–s19A); duration of authority and discharge (s20–s25); aftercare under supervision (s25A–s25J); functions of relatives of patients (s26–s30); supplemental (s31–s34).

- Part 3: Patients involved in criminal offences or under sentence, including remands to hospital (s35, s36); hospital and guardianship orders (s37–s40); restriction orders (s41–s45); hospital and limitation directions (s45A, s45B); detention during her Majesty's pleasure (s46); transfer to hospital of prisoners (s47–s53); supplemental (s54–s55).

- Part 4: Consent to treatment (s56–s64).

- Part 4A: Treatment of community patients not recalled to hospital (s64A–s64K).

- Part 5: Mental health review tribunals (s65–s79).

- Part 6: Removal and return of patients within the United Kingdom (s80–s92).

- Part 7: Management of property and affairs of patients (s93–s113).

- Part 8: Miscellaneous functions of local authority and secretary of state (s114–s125), which includes after care s117 (plans to replace Care Programme Approach with the Community Mental Health Framework).

- Part 9: Offences (s126–s130), which includes forgery/false statements (s126).

- Part 10: Miscellaneous and supplementary (s130A–s142B), which includes Independent Mental Health Advocates (s130A), and will be explained more in the next section.

2007 AMENDMENTS TO THE MENTAL HEALTH ACT 1983

One of the 2007 amendments to the MHA 1983 relates to the role of the Approved Mental Health Professional (AMHP), which was introduced to replace the role of the approved social worker. The change in the law enabled input from a wider range of professionals such as nurses and occupational therapists who undertook special training to enable them to work within this role (Lancashire and South Cumbria NHS Foundation Trust, 2021).

Another 2007 amendment to the MHA 1983 was for a person to have the right to an Independent Mental Health Advocate (IMHA). An IMHA is a specialist mental health advocate who can meet qualifying patients privately and consult with professionals concerned with the person's treatment and care (SCIE, 2014).

THE ROLE OF THE APPROVED MENTAL HEALTH PROFESSIONAL

Eligible professionals undertake the AMHP role on behalf of local authority social services departments, who are legally responsible for the AMHP service. The role is also closely linked to NHS MH Trusts, who provide many of the services that AMHPs require to undertake their role. AMHPs work in very close partnership with the NHS.

(Gov.UK, 2019, p 1)

The role of the AMHP includes working with the nearest relatives (MHA, 1983, s26), whose role is to protect and advocate for the rights of the person with a mental health issue. The nearest relative is a member of the person's family who has rights and responsibilities if a person is detained under sections 2, 3, 4 and 37 (Mind, 2020b). If a person does not have family who can act as the nearest relative, a friend or an AMHP can be appointed by the local county court (Mind, 2020b). The nearest relative can be displaced, which means if there are concerns about the way the nearest relative is behaving or the nearest relative no longer wants to be in the role, to apply for displacement an application can be made by an AMHP through the County Court (s29). The AMHP also needs to ensure appropriate interview methods are used when interviewing service users and that they know what their rights are if they are detained under the MHA 1983. The AMHP is usually the person that makes the applications for admission or guardianship (s13) in most MHA applications (Lancashire and South Cumbria NHS Foundation Trust, 2021).

Role of the AMHP in brief

○ AMHPs have a key statutory role in the effective delivery of mental health services.

○ AMHPs lead the organisation of statutory mental health assessments under the MHA 1983.

○   They are responsible for organising assessments, identifying the nearest relative and organising doctors and key agencies, such as police and the ambulance service.

○   AMHPs are independently responsible for a decision to detain a person and arrange conveyance to hospital.

○   AMHPs have a key responsibility to ensure that people's human rights are upheld and that the guiding principles of the MHA, as laid out in its Code of Practice: Mental Health Act 1983 (Gov.UK, 2015), are followed.

○   They ensure that the most appropriate legal framework is selected while at all times ensuring the least restrictive option is primary in the process (Gov.UK, 2019).

The AMHP also may at reasonable times enter and inspect any premises other than a hospital in which a person who experiences mental illness resides if they have reasonable cause to believe the service user is not being cared for appropriately (MHA 1983, s115). This could result in the AMHP presenting evidence to a Justice of the Peace (MHA 1983, s135) to obtain a warrant which will authorise the police, an AMHP, health professional and a registered medical practitioner to gain entry to the premises for an assessment to take place there, or for the person to be removed to a place of safety.

POLICE POWERS

Police have the power to detain if someone seems to be at risk of harming themselves or someone else. Under a section 135 warrant, the police have the powers to enter your home if there is a risk of harm and then a person may be taken to a place of safety for an assessment by an AMHP and a doctor (NHS, 2019b). If the police find a person in a public place and again they are at risk to themselves or others, and the person is in need of immediate care and control, the police have the power to take the person to a place of safety and detain them under section 136 for an assessment to be undertaken, again by an AMHP and a doctor; a person can be kept there for up to 24 hours (NHS, 2019b).

Main changes to police powers and places of safety

There have been some changes regarding police powers and places of safety within the MHA 1983 made by the Policing and Crime Act 2017, which include the following.

○   Section 136 powers may now be exercised anywhere other than in a private dwelling.

○   It is now unlawful for a police station to be used as a place of safety for anyone under the age of 18 in any circumstances.

○   A police station can now only be used as a place of safety for adults in explicit circumstances.

○   The previous maximum detention period was up to 72 hours; this has now been reduced to 24 hours (unless a doctor certifies that an extension of up to 12 hours is necessary).

○ Before exercising a section 136 (police power), police officers must, where feasible, consult one of the health professionals listed in section 136(1C), for example, an AMHP, registered nurse, registered medical practitioner, occupational therapist, paramedic (HPFT, 2018).

○ If a section 135 warrant has been issued, a person may be kept at their home (if it is a place of safety) for the purposes of an assessment rather than being removed to another place of safety.

○ There is also a new search power which allows police officers to search persons subject to section 135 or 136 powers for protective reasons.

(adapted from Department of Health and Home Office, 2017)

PERSONS WHO ARE IMPRISONED

The Centre for Mental Health, an independent charity which aims to help create a society in which people with mental health problems enjoy equal chances in life to those without mental health problems, wrote a report which explored '*pathways to unlocking secure mental health care*' (Centre for Mental Health, 2011) and examined '*the extent to which pathways into and through secure mental health services can be improved through the different security levels and ensure a better flow between prison and secure services*' (p 8). While we can only consider this report briefly in this chapter, you are encouraged to peruse this report to gain an understanding of forensic mental health. Secure mental health services, sometimes called forensic mental health services, refer to when people are imprisoned or are in hospital under the MHA 1983 following a criminal offence. The role of the social worker would involve assessment and care planning to ensure the best possible service is provided to the person experiencing mental health services, while at all times balancing choice with risk. Also advantageous is liaising with and accessing research conducted by charities such as the Centre for Mental Health to broaden knowledge and gain specialist understanding.

THE CARE PROGRAMME APPROACH AND COMMUNITY MENTAL HEALTH FRAMEWORK

If a person has been detained under section 3 (previously sectioned) of the MHA, section 117 requires health and social services to provide aftercare until those services are no longer required or they can be transferred to Care Programme Approach (CPA) (NHS, 2021). CPA is essential for people with serious mental illness as it supports them in the community, providing a care plan and preventing hospital admissions. Best social work practice is to apply the least restrictive options (Thomas et al, 2015) when working with people who experience mental health issues to enable them to live fuller, more empowering lives and prevent a person from being subject to sectioning. Using the least restrictive option would not mean putting a person at risk but rather, as far as is possible, encouraging the person to be able to access their interests, contribute to and engage in society and work towards their recovery goals.

CPA has had a central role in the planning and delivery of secondary care mental health services for almost 30 years (NHS, 2019c). The principles underlying the CPA are sound and there has been some excellent work over the years in implementing and improving it. However, the Community Mental Health Framework (CMHF) is planned to replace the Care Programme Approach in the future. Although the principles are maintained and the CMHF is still a package of care for people with mental health problems, the changes include that the framework will be applicable to people irrespective of their diagnosis, which includes conditions such as

> ...coexisting frailty (likely in older adults), coexisting neurodevelopmental conditions, eating disorders, common mental health problems, such as anxiety or depression, complex mental health difficulties associated with a diagnosis of personality dis- order, co-occurring drug or alcohol-use disorders, and other addiction problems, including gambling problems and severe mental illnesses such as psychosis or bipolar disorder.
>
> (NHS, 2019c, p 7)

Some of the key aims of the CMHF are that people with mental health problems will be 'enabled as active participants in making positive changes' rather than passive recipients of care and that good mental health care, support and treatment will be delivered in the community (NHS, 2019c, p 8).

COMMUNITY TREATMENT ORDER (MENTAL HEALTH ACT 1983, S17A)

It is important for you to understand what a community treatment order (CTO) is and what it means for the person subject to it, to be able to support them in a person-centred way. If a person has been detained and treated in hospital, when they go back into the community they may be discharged on a CTO, which is made by the person's Responsible Clinician (RC) (Mind, 2020c). Although what this effectively means is that a person can be treated in the community for their mental health condition, the RC also has the power to admit the person back to hospital for immediate treatment if it is deemed necessary to do so.

A CTO is a legal order made by the Mental Health Review Tribunal or by a magistrate. It sets out the terms under which a person must accept medication and therapy, counsel-ling, management, rehabilitation and other services while living in the community (Mind, 2020c). There are conditions attached to the CTO, which may be that the person needs to reside at a certain address, attend appointments for treatment, see the RC when asked to and be compliant with seeing a second opinion doctor if they are asked to do so (Mind, 2020c). If a person is subject to a section 3 (previously sectioned), section 37 (hospital order) or section 47 (unrestricted transfer direction), they can be put on a CTO; if a person is subject to section 2 (first section), section 4 (compulsory admission) or section 5 (prevents discharge from hospital) or if they have been discharged they still need to be on a section to be put on a CTO (Mind, 2020c). The CTO lasts six months and can be renewed by the RC.

If the conditions of the CTO are not met it could result in the person being admitted back to hospital for assessment and/or treatment or the CTO being revoked and the person being detained in hospital. If a person wants to be discharged from their CTO, they need to apply to the Mental Health Tribunal (s65–s79) and when they can apply would depend on which section they are subject to. However, the tribunal will consider the person's current mental condition; a person is able to ask for an Independent Mental Health Advocate to support them in this process (Mind, 2020c).

MENTAL HEALTH AND CHILDREN

It could be argued that all young children are curtailed of their liberty due to their tender age (Thomas et al, 2015). However, Public Health England highlight that '*Around half of all lifetime mental health problems start by the mid-teens, and three-quarters by the mid-20s, although treatment typically does not start until a number of years later*' (2019, p 1). The NHS (2018) conducted a survey, finding the following key facts.

○   One in eight (12.8 per cent) children aged 5–19 years had at least one mental disorder when assessed in 2017.

○   Specific mental disorders were grouped into four broad categories: emotional, behavioural, hyperactivity and other less common disorders. Emotional disorders were found to be the most predominant type of disorder experienced by children and young people aged 5–19 years in 2017 (8.1 per cent).

○   Rates of mental disorders increased with age; 5.5 percent of children aged 2–4 years experienced a mental disorder, compared to 16.9 per cent of young people aged 17–19. The survey highlighted that caution is needed when comparing rates between age groups due to differences in data collection. For example, teacher reports were available only for children aged 5–6 years.

○   Data from this survey series reveals a slight increase over time in the prevalence of mental disorders in children and young people aged 5–15 years (the age group covered on all surveys in this series): rising from 9.7 per cent in 1999 and 10.1 per cent in 2004, to 11.2 per cent in 2017.

○   Emotional disorders have become more prevalent in children and young people aged 5–15, going from 4.3 per cent in 1999 and 3.9 per cent in 2004 to 5.8 per cent in 2017. All other types of disorder, such as behavioural, hyperactivity and other less common disorders, have remained similar in prevalence for this age group since 1999.

(adapted from NHS, 2018)

As well as these statistics Public Health England (2019) highlight that poor mental well-being in children and young people can lead to an increased likelihood of poor educational attainment, risk of teenage pregnancy, risk of drug and alcohol misuse, anti-social behaviour, and involvement in criminal activity. Therefore, it is apparent that social workers will at some time in their working career work with children who experience mental health problems and thus you need to understand mental health legislation relevant to working with children. For the purpose of this section, we are going to look at application of section 2 of the MHA 1983 in relation to a case study, as outlined by Thomas et al (2015).

Case study

B was an eight year-old boy admitted to a child and adolescent mental health in-patient unit as an emergency because of extremely challenging behaviour. B has mental disorder (autism spectrum disorder and hyperkinetic conduct disorder) and was presenting in a way that put his own safety, and that of others, at risk.

Firstly, it is important to say that, as highlighted by Thomas et al (2015), detention of a young child is unusual and a last resort since where possible the least restrictive option would be applied. Also, children who are considered to be Gillick competent (can consent to their own treatment) can make decisions themselves; otherwise the adult with parental responsibility (Children Act 1989, s3, rights, power, responsibilities) would contribute to decisions (Thomas et al, 2015), unless it was deemed that it was not in the best interests of the child for them to do so (eg child protection). In the case study, since B was a risk to himself and others, '*following a Mental Health Act assessment and close consultation with local authority and trust legal services, B was detained under section 2*' (Thomas et al, 2015, p 304) of the MHA 1983.

Also, bear in mind the following:

> If a child is subject to a care order or emergency protection order under the Children Act 1989, the local authority acquires parental responsibility (Children Act 1989 s 33(3)(a) and s 44(4)(c), respectively). Section 25 of the Children Act 1989 can be used to detain a person with mental disorder under a secure accommodation order, but only if the primary purpose of detention is not to provide treatment for mental disorder, for example, if detention is required to maintain the safety of someone who exhibits severe behavioural disturbance.
>
> (Thomas et al, 2015, p 3)

THE ROLE OF THE SOCIAL WORKER WHEN WORKING WITH CHILDREN AND THEIR PARENT(S)/CAREGIVERS

Although the child may be receiving clinical treatment/support where possible, the social worker needs to support both the parents/caregivers and the child to provide holistic support. Although support services will be different in different areas, perhaps you can signpost the child and/or the parent(s)/caregiver to:

○ parenting support for parents/caregivers – parenting programmes through local authorities and support from charitable organisations;

○ child support through support programmes available in your local area and trusts such as the Prince's Trust (for more information, see Prince's Trust, 2022).

DUTIES AND RESPONSIBILITIES OF THE SOCIAL WORKER

Social workers who work in mental health services, even if they are not trained AMHPs, need to understand legislation that affects people with mental health problems to enable best-possible practice. When a service user is detained (MHA 1983, s2, s3) or treated as a result of mental health legislation, it is probably at a time of their life that they are at a low point, feeling vulnerable and out of control; the care and support offered by a social worker can make a difference. However, social workers also need to ensure they protect their own mental health and well-being and practise safely, especially when lone working, ensuring they follow organisational policies, protocols and procedures and when issues arise talking to their line manager and senior managers. It is also important for social workers to read referrals to obtain information to see if the person's mental health experience is historical (in the past) or clinical (active). An important aspect of social work practice is to accurately record details of work with service users/experts by experience, which enables another practitioner to have up-to-date records and have a comprehensive picture of the person with whom they are working.

THE MENTAL HEALTH ACT 1983 IN BRIEF

○ First section (s2).

○ Previously sectioned (s3).

○ Prevents discharge from hospital (s5).

○ Nearest relative (s26).

○ Informal admission (s131).

○ Police powers (s136).

THE MENTAL HEALTH ACT 2007 (AMENDMENTS) IN BRIEF

○ The change in the law enabled input from a wider range of professionals such as nurses and occupational therapists to work as an AMHP.

○ Introduced role of IMHA.

DECISIONS MADE ON CASE STUDIES

To enable you to see how decisions were made see below.

Ava

The police and the AMHP managed to get Ava's mum on video conferencing and as Ava spoke to her mum she calmed down. This resulted in Ava agreeing to an informal admission to hospital (s131); this was better for Ava since she went to hospital in a calmer way. Once in hospital, because she had not been sectioned or detained previously, she was sectioned under section 2 of the MHA. Ava was encouraged to speak to her mum again on video conferencing, resulting in Ava asking if her mum could be her nearest relative (s26), which again contributed to calming Ava.

As with the case study of Ava, just because a person has a mental health condition does not mean that everything should not be done to try to talk to the person and encourage them to agree to informal admissions (MHA 1983, s131) to hospital. Although the pandemic has brought much misery and heartache, it has also opened up technology and with today's technology, professionals and family support can be provided via platforms such as video conferencing. As with Ava, if a person can speak to a familiar loved one, it can make all the difference with their anxiety levels.

B

B was deemed a risk to himself and others, following an MHA assessment and consultation with local authority and trust legal services; B was detained under section 2 of the MHA 1983.

The case study of B highlights that a child can be detained under the MHA 1983 but the least restrictive option should always apply where possible.

Key points to remember

Remember that where possible the least restrictive option should always be applied. Also, although the MHA 1983 and the 2007 amendment are complex areas of legislation, you do not need to memorise every single section, but just have a sound foundation knowledge of it. The important point is to understand how to access information when you need it, for example by looking at government guidelines and specialist organisations and working with other professionals and experts by experience who have greater knowledge and wider experience.

TEST YOUR LEGISLATIVE KNOWLEDGE

Answers are at the back of the book.

Questions

- What is section 2?

- What is section 3?

- What is section 26?

- What does s117 require?

- Which two roles were introduced under the 2007 amendment of the MHA 1983?

CHAPTER SUMMARY

In this chapter, we have considered the MHA 1983/2007 in the context of social work practice and highlighted its importance with regard to assessing, treating and upholding the rights of people who experience mental health issues. The case studies of Ava and B enabled you to see how although the MHA is there to protect people with mental illness, as in the case of Ava where possible the least restrictive option should be applied. Mental health was considered in a variety of settings, children and adults as well as persons imprisoned. As we have not been able to cover every aspect of mental health, you are encouraged to conduct further research yourselves, perhaps using the references provided in the reference list as a starting point.

END OF CHAPTER ACTIVITY TO CAPTURE PERSONAL REFLECTIONS AND INDIVIDUAL THOUGHTS

Critically reflect on this chapter and what you have learned, recording your own personal thoughts and feelings; as in previous chapters, use the mindmap to assist you. The reflective model you might like to consider in this chapter is Maclean's (2020) component model of reflection. Also, as in previous chapters consider if there are any anti-discriminatory or anti-oppressive practice issues (Equality Act 2010) that stand out for you.

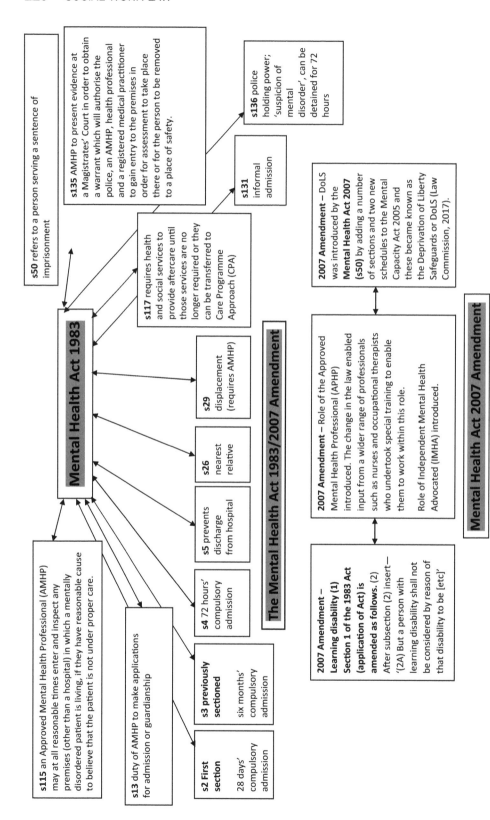

s115 an Approved Mental Health Professional (AMHP) may at all reasonable times enter and inspect any premises (other than a hospital) in which a mentally disordered patient is living, if they have reasonable cause to believe that the patient is not under proper care.

s135 AMHP to present evidence at a Magistrates' Court in order to obtain a warrant which will authorise the police, an AMHP, health professional and a registered medical practitioner to gain entry to the premises in order for assessment to take place there or for the person to be removed to a place of safety.

s50 refers to a person serving a sentence of imprisonment

s136 police holding power; 'suspicion of mental disorder', can be detained for 72 hours

s131 informal admission

Mental Health Act 1983

s117 requires health and social services to provide aftercare until those services are no longer required or they can be transferred to Care Programme Approach (CPA)

s13 duty of AMHP to make applications for admission or guardianship

s29 displacement (requires AMHP)

s26 nearest relative

s5 prevents discharge from hospital

s4 72 hours' compulsory admission

s3 previously sectioned
six months' compulsory admission

s2 First section
28 days' compulsory admission

The Mental Health Act 1983/2007 Amendment

2007 Amendment – Role of the Approved Mental Health Professional (APHP) introduced. The change in the law enabled input from a wider range of professionals such as nurses and occupational therapists who undertook special training to enable them to work within this role.

Role of Independent Mental Health Advocated (IMHA) introduced.

2007 Amendment – DoLS was introduced by the **Mental Health Act 2007** (**s50**) by adding a number of sections and two new schedules to the Mental Capacity Act 2005 and these became known as the Deprivation of Liberty Safeguards or DoLS (Law Commission, 2017).

2007 Amendment – Learning disability **(1)** Section 1 of the 1983 Act (application of Act) is amended as follows. (2) After subsection (2) insert— '(2A) But a person with learning disability shall not be considered by reason of that disability to be [etc]'

Mental Health Act 2007 Amendment

Capture your personal reflections and individual thoughts here

REFERENCES

Centre for Mental Health (2011) *Pathways to Unlocking Secure Mental Health*. [online] Available at: www.centreformentalhealth.org.uk/sites/default/files/2018-09/Pathways_to_unlocking_secure_mental_health_care.pdf (accessed 14 December 2021).

Department of Health and Home Office (2017) *Guidance for the Implementation of Changes to Police Powers and Places of Safety Provision in the Mental Health Act 1983*. [online] Available at: https://assets.publishing.service.gov.uk/government/uploads/system/uploads/attachment_data/file/656025/Guidance_on_Police_Powers.PDF (accessed 14 December 2021).

Department of Health and Social Care (2021) Reforming the Mental Health Act – Joint Foreword from the Secretary of State for Health and Social Care and the Secretary of State for Justice and Lord Chancellor. [online] Available at: www.gov.uk/government/consultations/reforming-the-mental-health-act/reforming-the-mental-health-act (accessed 15 December 2021).

Equality Act 2010 [online] Available at: www.legislation.gov.uk/ukpga/2010/15/contents (accessed 4 March 2022).

Gov.UK (2015) Code of Practice: Mental Health Act 1983. [online] Available at: www.gov.uk/government/publications/code-of-practice-mental-health-act-1983 (accessed 15 December 2021).

Gov.UK (2019) National Workforce Plan for Approved Mental Health Professionals (AMHPs). [online] Available at: www.gov.uk/government/publications/national-workforce-plan-for-approved-mental-health-professionals-amhps (accessed 14 December 2021).

Hertfordshire Partnership University NHS Foundation Trust (HPFT) (2018) *Managing a Place of Safety Detention Under Section 136 of the Mental Health Act 1983*. [online] Available at: www.hpft.nhs.uk/media/4633/mha-managing-a-place-of-safety-s136-policy.pdf (accessed 15 December 2021).

Lancashire and South Cumbria NHS Foundation Trust (2021) What is an Approved Mental Health Professional? [online] Available at: www.lscft.nhs.uk/Approved-Mental-Health-Professional (accessed 16 December 2021).

Law Commission (2017) Mental Capacity and Deprivation of Liberty. [online] Available at: www.lawcom.gov.uk/app/uploads/2017/03/lcmentalcapacity.pdf (accessed 26 April 2022).

Maclean, S (2020) Component Models of Reflection. [online] Available at: www.youtube.com/watch?v=_1w4AyRNFDU (accessed 14 December 2021).

Marshal, L, Bibby, J and Abbs, I (2020) Emerging Evidence on COVID-19's Impact on Mental Health and Health Inequalities. The Health Foundation. [online] Available at: www.health.org.uk/news-and-comment/blogs/emerging-evidence-on-covid-19s-impact-on-mental-health-and-health (accessed 4 March 2022).

Mental Health Act 1983 [online] Available at: www.legislation.gov.uk/ukpga/1983/20/contents (accessed 15 December 2021).

Mental Health Act 2007 [online] Available at: www.legislation.gov.uk/ukpga/2007/12/contents (accessed 14 December 2021).

Mind (2020a) How Common are Mental Health Problems? [online] Available at: www.mind.org.uk/information-support/types-of-mental-health-problems/statistics-and-facts-about-mental-health/how-common-are-mental-health-problems (accessed 4 March 2022).

Mind (2020b) Nearest Relative. [online] Available at: www.mind.org.uk/information-support/legal-rights/nearest-relative/about-the-nearest-relative (accessed 14 December 2021).

Mind (2020c) Community Treatment Orders (CTOs). [online] Available at: www.mind.org.uk/information-support/legal-rights/community-treatment-orders-ctos/overview (accessed 15 December 2021).

Murphy, G (2019) Whorlton Hall: A Predictable Tragedy? *BMJ*, 2019: 366.

NHS (2018) Mental Health of Children and Young People in England, 2017. [online] Available at: https://digital.nhs.uk/data-and-information/publications/statistical/mental-health-of-children-and-young-people-in-england/2017/2017 (accessed 15 December 2021).

NHS (2019a) *Mental Health Implementation Plan 2019/20 – 2023/24.* [online] Available at: www.longtermplan.nhs.uk/publication/nhs-mental-health-implementation-plan-2019-20-2023-24 (accessed 15 December 2021).

NHS (2019b) Mental Health Act. [online] Available at: www.nhs.uk/mental-health/social-care-and-your-rights/mental-health-and-the-law/mental-health-act (accessed 17 December 2021).

NHS (2019c) *The Community Mental Health Framework for Adults and Older Adults* [online] Available at: www.england.nhs.uk/wp-content/uploads/2019/09/community-mental-health-framework-for-adults-and-older-adults.pdf (accessed 15 December 2021).

NHS (2021) Care Programme Approach [online] Available at: www.england.nhs.uk/wp-content/uploads/2021/07/Care-Programme-Approach-Position-Statement_FINAL_2021.pdf (accessed 15 December 2021).

Policing and Crime Act 2017 [online] Available at: www.legislation.gov.uk/ukpga/2017/3/section/80/enacted (accessed 14 December 2021).

Prince's Trust 2022 Start Something: Help for Young People. [online] Available at: www.princes-trust.org.uk/help-for-young-people/who-else/housing-health-wellbeing/wellbeing/mental-health (accessed 30 March 2022).

Public Health England (2019) JSNA Toolkit: Children and Young People. [online] Available at: www.gov.uk/government/publications/better-mental-health-jsna-toolkit/5-children-and-young-people (accessed 15 December 2021).

Social Care Institute for Excellence (SCIE) (2014) Independent Mental Health Advocacy (IMHA). [online] Available at: www.scie.org.uk/independent-mental-health-advocacy/resources-for-staff/understanding (accessed 15 December 2021).

Thomas, V, Chipchase, B, Rippon, L and McArdle, P (2015) The Application of Mental Health Legislation in Younger Children. *BJPsych Bulletin*, 39(6): 302–4.

9   Legislation pertaining to disability/impairment seen and unseen

INTRODUCTION

In this chapter, legislation pertaining to disability/impairment seen and unseen will be considered in the context of application to practice. For the purpose of this chapter, the discussion relating to children and young people will consider physical, learning and sensory impairment/disability. The discussion relating to legislation with adults will primarily focus on sensory impairment/disability. There will also be a discussion relating to the differences between small 'd' and capital 'D' D/deafness/D/deafblindness. The case study of Qi will explore seen impairment/disability and when a child is transitioning from child to adult services, while the case study of Alonzo will consider legislation when working with unseen impairment/disability. Reference will be made to the Equality Act 2010, Human Rights Act 1998, Care Act 2014, Local Authority and Social Services Act 1970, Children Act 1989/2004 and the Children and Families Act 2014 in relation to disability/impairment to enable readers to see how a range of legislative options can work in harmony with each other to support people that need service provision as a result of disability/impairment.

The Equality Act 2010 defines a person as disabled if they have a physical or mental impairment that has a substantial and long-term negative effect on their ability to do normal daily activities (s6, Gov.UK, 2010). However, the term disability has been debated by disability campaigners who have raised awareness, identifying the differences between disability and impairment. It is essential for you to understand these differences to be able to apply legislation effectively to provide individualised support for the people with whom you are working. Shakespeare (1992) suggests that disability campaigners severed the link between the physical body and the social situation so, for example, impairment is bodily or biological, while disability is societal or a social circumstance where it is not the impairment itself that disables people but society which disables people with impairments (Hughes and Paterson, 1997; Evans, 2019; Jenks, 2019; Evans and Baillie, 2021).

The Union of the Physically Impaired Against Segregation (UPIAS) was 'founded by (Paul) Hunt' in the 1970s (Beckett and Campbell, 2015, p 271). The document 'Principles of Disability' highlighted that:

> Disability is something imposed on top of our impairments by the way we are unnecessarily isolated and excluded from full participation in society. Disabled people are therefore an oppressed group in society.
>
> (UPIAS, 1976, p 4)

Sometimes disabilities are evident, for example a person may have mobility difficulties and use a wheelchair; however, some impairments/disabilities are unseen or '*non-apparent impairments*' (Evans, 2019, p 726), such as kidney disease (Ofori-Ansah et al, 2021), autism, acquired brain injury, cancer, mental health issues and sensory impairment such as D/deafness and D/deafblindness (Evans, 2018a, p 2). As an example, if a person with Usher syndrome (a rare form of congenital/hereditary deafblindness) is not using a red and white cane to indicate they have hearing and sight difficulties, they could be perceived as being hearing and sighted and the services they may need will not be considered. However, if the person does use the cane, research shows that this can lead to feelings of vulnerability as the cane identifies them as deafblind (Evans, 2018b). Thus, when social workers work with people with impairments/disabilities, disability diversity and each individual's need must be taken into account; this individualised support can be provided by understanding and applying legislation effectively.

As previously identified (Chapter 7), a social worker is required to be registered and is regulated by Social Work England (2021); thus, understanding legislation applicable to working with people who experience different and diverse seen and unseen disabilities is essential. Depending on your personal or secular experiences, you may not have come into contact with people who experience impairment/disability or be able to recognise impairment/disability. Alternatively, if you do have experience, you may have had bad experiences or not known how to work with someone with a disability/impairment. This chapter raises awareness and provides you with the knowledge to practise supportively, empoweringly and effectively within a legislative framework.

Two case studies will be considered in the context of legislation applicable to people who experience seen and unseen impairment – Qi and Alonzo.

Case study

Qi (means enlightenment; wondrous) is 17 years-old. Qi's parents were both born in China and speak Chinese and English fluently; Qi was born in the UK. Qi has a mild learning disability and was diagnosed with Duchenne muscular dystrophy (DMD), a hereditary disorder which involves muscle weakness at birth, and uses a wheelchair due to mobility issues; his impairment/disability is seen. Qi was receiving services from the children with disabilities team, but has recently moved home to a different area. His previous social worker, Blessing, has referred Qi to the new local authority. Once Qi reaches 18 years of age, he will need adult service provision. Blessing has requested the transition assessment to be conducted as soon as possible so there is no gap in support for Qi and his family.

Case study

Alonzo is 22 years-old and was born in Spain but has lived in the UK since he was a child. Alonzo has experienced hearing loss and worn hearing aids since childhood but recently he found his hearing had deteriorated and that he was struggling to see well at night. After consultation with audiology (hearing) and ophthalmology (sight), Alonzo was diagnosed with Usher syndrome (D/deafblindness). Alonzo lives with his mum, who is hearing and verbally communicates with him as Alonzo lipreads (where a person who is D/deafblind reads the lips of another person to receive information conveyed). Alonzo wears tinted contact lenses to reduce glare and invisible hearing aids, which are very small and cannot be seen on the outside of the ear; his impairment/disability is unseen.

LEGISLATION PERTAINING TO CHILDREN AND YOUNG PEOPLE WHO EXPERIENCE IMPAIRMENT/DISABILITY

As with adults, disability is a protected characteristic under the Equality Act 2010 (s4) for children and young people and the Act sets out legal rights for children and their families. The Equality Act only applies if the child's disability is permanent, so for example if the child has an ear infection, unless it lasts for 12 months or more, then that child is not eligible for support under the Equality Act (NDCS, 2020).

Although not all children may identify as being disabled, conditions including experiencing sensory impairment such as d/Deafness/d/Deafblindness/visual impairment, being on the autistic spectrum, or having attention deficit hyperactivity disorder (ADHD), a learning disability, a physical disability such as DMD or a long-term illness may be referred to as disabilities (NDCS, 2021).

Children and young people with a range of disabilities/impairments including d/Deafness are also eligible for services under the Children Act 1989 section 17 because they are a child in need. Should risk of significant harm arise they are safeguarded under the Children Act 1989 (s47) with the Children Act 2004 s11 making it clear that a range of organisations, agencies and individuals have duties to protect and safeguard children. The National Deaf Children Society (NDCS) also provides guidance on how to protect d/Deaf and disabled children and young people from abuse (NDCS, 2021).

The Children and Families Act 2014 brought together social care, health and education to better support children and young people with special education needs and disabilities (SEND) and their families with support such as personal budgets and a single assessment process which ensures the child is involved in what is happening to them and that their voice is heard and recorded (NSPCC, 2021).

The section of the Children and Families Act 2014 that relates to children and young people with disabilities/impairments is part 3, specifically sections 19–83. Although not all 64 sections will be covered in detail in this chapter, you are encouraged to explore the various sections to give you a greater understanding of how to apply the Children and Families Act 2014 in practice.

Children – seen impairment/disability

To give you an idea of how the Equality Act 2010 and the Children and Families Act 2014 work in practice, sections 22, 24 and 32 will be considered in the context of the case study of Qi. As Qi has DMD (Muscular Dystrophy UK, 2021) and a mild learning disability (Williams and Evans, 2013), he would be eligible for protection against discrimination under the Equality Act 2010 (s4). Although, section 22 of the Children and Families Act 2014 outlines that local authorities need to identify children and young people with SEND in their area to ascertain support that may be provided, the case study highlights that the family have just moved into the area and have been referred by their previous social worker. Qi has special educational needs and identifies as disabled; therefore, as section 24 highlights, the local authority has responsibilities for him and he is allocated a social worker (Jude) from the children with disabilities team in the area in which he now lives. Section 32 relates to advice and information; therefore, the local authority would have a responsibility to provide Qi and his parents with advice and information about matters relating to his special educational needs and disabilities in formats accessible to Qi and his parents. The case study mentioned that Qi, although currently receiving services from the children with disabilities team, is now 17 years of age and will soon transition to adult services; in the next section we will see how this works in practice when working with Qi.

LEGISLATION PERTAINING TO IMPAIRMENT SEEN AND UNSEEN IN THE CONTEXT OF APPLICATION TO PRACTICE WHEN A CHILD IS TRANSITIONING FROM CHILD TO ADULT SERVICES

Chapter 6 highlighted the importance of smooth transitioning from children to adult services to ensure there is no gap in support for children, young people and their families/carers (Mencap, 2021). Chapter 10 will also outline the sections (s58–s66) of the Care Act 2014 that apply to transition from children to adult care and support. Social workers should also take into account the need to respect the service user's and their family's human rights (Human Rights Act 1998) and assist them to express their wishes and feelings (Equality Act 2010) when transitioning takes place.

Whether the child's disability/impairment is seen or unseen, all children should be supported with needs they may have. For example, if a child and their family are Deaf and their first language is British Sign Language (BSL, an official language in its own right using signs with its own grammatical structure, syntax and regional variances), an interpreter should be sought to ensure that the child and their family are involved in all aspects of the transition process. If the child or their parent(s)/carer(s) has a physical disability, interview rooms need to be considered to ensure they are accessible to everyone. The social worker should at all times consider the child's welfare as paramount (Children Act 1989, s1) and due consideration should be given to the child's wishes and feelings (Children Act 2004, s53) while at all times safeguarding them (Children Act 1989, s47).

Returning to the case study of Qi, Jude, Qi's social worker, would co-ordinate and work with the adult transition social worker to arrange a meeting with Qi and his parents to discuss the process. Due to Qi's physical disability, Jude would need to ensure accessible interview rooms or a home visit was arranged as well as information and advice in a format that was understandable for Qi. Remember, although Qi is being assessed for adult services, he is still currently a child and therefore child legislation (Children Act 1989/2004; Children and Families Act 2014) applies. Once he has reached 18 years of age and considered eligible for adult services, then adult legislation (Care Act 2014) would apply. Qi would be assessed for transitional care and support under the Care Act 2014 (s58) and his parents (carers) offered an assessment (s60).

WORKING WITH PEOPLE WITH SENSORY IMPAIRMENT/ DISABILITY: UNDERSTANDING THE DIFFERENCE BETWEEN SMALL 'd' AND CAPITAL d/DEAFBLINDNESS

When working with d/Deaf or d/Deafblind people it is important for social workers to understand the difference between small d and capital D d/Deaf and d/Deafblindness as it impacts access to services and equitable and individualised care.

Capital 'D' Deafness refers to a person who considers themselves to be culturally Deaf (Evans, 2018b). The person would most likely be a profoundly Deaf person who would not consider themselves to be disabled, but rather part of a minority group with its own culture, history and linguistics (British Deaf Association, 2015). Deaf people consider being Deaf as part of their heritage and most likely consider themselves proud to be Deaf (Evans and Whittaker, 2010; Evans, 2018b). Deafblind with a capital 'D' refers to people who consider themselves to be culturally Deaf but also experience sight loss (Evans, 2018b; Evans and Baillie, 2021).

> *Small 'd' deafness refers to a person who is likely to have been previously a hearing person or one who was born deaf, growing up in a hearing family with oral communication being the primary means of communication and they would most likely consider deafness to be a disability. People, who are deaf and then experience sight loss, are referred to as deafblind and again will most likely consider their sensory loss to be a disability.*
>
> (Evans, 2018b, p 1)

It is important therefore to gain insight as to what impairment/disability means to the people with whom you will be working.

ADULTS' UNSEEN IMPAIRMENT/DISABILITY

Legislation pertaining to impairment unseen will next be applied in the context of the case study of Alonzo. Alonzo grew up in a hearing family with the primary means of communication being oral, and considers being diagnosed with Usher syndrome to be a disability (small 'd' deafness). Alonzo is now experiencing Usher syndrome (D/deafblindness) and he needs more support with daily practical activities. The Care Act 2014 (CA), particularly Part 1 (s1–s80), could be used to support him. Most likely in this scenario either the audiologist or the ophthalmologist or both would have referred Alonzo to a Sensory Services Team and a social worker would be allocated to conduct an assessment under section 9 of the CA 2014. If it transpired Alonzo met the eligibility criteria (CA, s13), services and support may be provided. A carer's assessment (CA, s10) would also be conducted with his mum (if she consented). Direct payments (CA, s31–s33) may be a good option to consider for Alonzo as this would enable him to retain his independence (for more information on the Care Act 2014, see Chapter 10).

ADULTS' SEEN IMPAIRMENT/DISABILITY

As highlighted earlier, when working with people who experience D/deafness/D/deafblindness, social workers first need to understand if an individual considers themselves to have an impairment or a disability (Evans, 2017) to ensure individualised service provision. Although some impairment is seen, the person experiencing the impairment may not consider themselves to be disabled, for example a person whose first language is BSL and who is culturally Deaf. Although a person who experiences D/deafness is entitled to an assessment under the Care Act 2014 (s9) and if considered eligible (s13) would be provided with services provision, Hardy (2018) highlights that Deaf people whose first language is BSL may have reduced opportunities for direct communication and while interpreters are bound by codes of practice, other people are not. For example, Hardy (2018, p 2) notes that '*if someone else is always the gatekeeper of information and communicative transactions, they may exert unacceptable levels of control or frank exploitation of another*'.

D/deaf people, whether they use signed or verbal communication, may also have reduced opportunities to report concerns; this combined with lack of d/Deaf awareness can create barriers when reporting (Hardy, 2018). Older people too can be at risk if they are in non-signing environments; for example, they may not have access to sensory equipment such as doorbells (eg flashing doorbells) and fire alarms. Finally, Hardy posits that '*poor access to information and communication over a lifetime may result in deaf people being less aware than the general population of a range of issues including abuse and safeguarding*' (2018, p 2). Taking into account the vulnerabilities and uniqueness when working with people with sensory requirement/need highlights the importance of social workers understanding legislation to be able to apply person-centred practice. Although as discussed in Chapter 10, the Care Act 2014 section 42 places a duty on local authorities to make enquiries where a person is at risk of abuse and/or neglect, the local authority has to be aware of it in the first place.

CHILDREN AND ADULTS WHO EXPERIENCE D/DEAFBLINDNESS

The D/deafblind guidance is 'Care and Support for Deafblind Children and Adults' (Department of Health, 2014). This guidance is *'issued jointly under section 7 of the Local Authority Social Services Act 1970 in relation to children, and section 78 of the Care Act 2014 in relation to adults'* (Department of Health, 2014, p 4). The Care Act 2014 provides frameworks for adult care and support with sections 77 and 78 explaining how local authorities should determine who is eligible for support and provide this support where appropriate (Sense, 2020). Section 7 of the 1970 Act outlines provision with respect to the organisation, management and administration of local authority social services for children (Sense, 2020).

The Department of Health (2014) guidance indicates how local authorities should act when providing care and support for people who experience d/Deafblindness (Sense, 2020). For example, local authorities should identify, make contact with and keep records of people in their area who experience d/Deafblindness and, when they do, ensure the assessment is individualised and conducted by someone who has specific training and expertise relating to d/Deafblindness. Information should be provided in an accessible format for d/Deafblind people and a director-level local authority representative should assume overall responsibility for d/Deafblind services (Sense, 2020).

DUTIES AND RESPONSIBILITIES OF THE SOCIAL WORKER

If a person is experiencing disability seen or unseen and requires support, a referral can be made to the local authority to request an assessment of need (child: Children Act 1989, s17; adult: Care Act 2014, s9); it is at this point that the social worker becomes involved. If a specialist sensory assessment (child: Local Authority and Social Services Act 1970, s7; adult: Care Act 2014, s77) is required, the social worker should have appropriate skills to effectively communicate and understand individual needs. Although it is not always possible for social workers to have specialist knowledge and skills depending on which demographic areas they work within (some may be remote, with small numbers of inhabitants), the social worker should always research the impairments/disabilities of the people they are working with, so for example with the case study of Qi, they should research what it is like to live with DMD. The carer's assessment is also vital (Qi's parents: Children and Families Act 2014; Alonzo's mum: Care Act 2014) to ensure holistic support is provided.

It is important for social workers to understand how different and unique individuals can be and tailor their services to support them; this could include working in partnership with charities and organisations such as Sense, a national charitable organisation for people who are deafblind, and whose focus is to support and campaign for children and adults who are deafblind (Evans, 2018b).

BRIEF SUMMARY OF LEGISLATION USED IN THIS CHAPTER IN RELATION TO DISABILITY

○ Equality Act 2010: Section 6 provides the definition of disability, which is that a person is disabled if they have a physical or mental impairment that has a substantial long-term effect on their ability to do normal daily activities.

○ Human Rights Act 1998: Respect service users' and their families' human rights.

○ Care Act 2014: Sections 77 and 78 explain how local authorities should determine who is eligible for support and provide support where appropriate.

○ Local Authority and Social Services Act 1970: Section 7 outlines provision with respect to the organisation, management and administration of local authority social services for children who experience d/Deafblindness.

○ Children Act 1989: Section 1 welfare of the child is paramount; also section 17 child in need, section 47 child is at risk of significant harm.

○ 2004 amendment of the Children Act 1989: Section 53, due consideration to child's wishes and feelings.

○ Children and Families Act 2014: Part 3, which includes sections 19–83 relates to children and young people with special educational needs and disabilities/impairments.

DECISIONS MADE ON CASE STUDIES

To enable you to see how the decisions were made see below.

The case study relating to Qi

The case study of Qi was an example of a seen disability as he has DMD. Initially the importance of social work referral was highlighted because if a service user is moving to a different area, handover can make a big difference in preventing gaps in service for people in need. Once the case has been allocated to another social worker, it was evident Qi was eligible for services because under the Equality Act 2010 he was considered to have a disability/impairment (s6). As under the Children and Families Act 2014 (s22, 24) the local authority has a responsibility for Qi, an assessment would be conducted to consider services to meet his needs. As Qi also has a mild learning disability, advice and information about matters relating to SEND would be provided by the local authority (s32).

The case study relating to Alonzo

This was an example of unseen disability/impairment, as not all sensory impairment/disability is visible. As Alonzo is now experiencing Usher syndrome, he needs more support with daily practical activities and can be supported with this under the Care Act 2014. After the social worker conducted an assessment (s9), it transpired Alonzo met the eligibility criteria (s13). A carer's assessment (s10) was also offered to his mum. As Alonzo wanted to retain his independence as far as possible, direct payments (s31–s33) were arranged to enable Alonzo to fund practical support.

Key points to remember

Legislation pertaining to disability both seen and unseen can at first seem complex as there is no single piece of legislation to refer to for guidance but rather several. A useful point of contact can be specialist organisations, such as Sense, who work with people who experience D/deafblindness and therefore have specialist knowledge relating to D/deafblindness, or the NDCS, who work with children who experience Deafness and their families/carers and therefore have specialist knowledge in this area; sources such as these are often a rich source of knowledge.

TEST YOUR LEGISLATIVE KNOWLEDGE

Answers are at the back of the book.

Questions

- Which Act and which section gives the definition of disability?

- Which Act protects service users' and their families' human rights?

- Which sections of the Care Act 2014 explain how local authorities should determine who is eligible for support and provide support where appropriate?

- Which Act would you use to support children who experience D/deafblindness?

- Which Act and section would you use to a) promote the welfare of a child, b) support a child with a disability and c) safeguard a child?

- Which section of the 2004 amendment to the Children Act 1989 would you use to consider the child's wishes and feelings?

- Which Act and which part relates to children and young people with special educational needs and disabilities/impairments?

CHAPTER SUMMARY

In summary, this chapter explored various Acts and guidance that social workers need to be aware of when working with children and adults with disabilities/impairment both seen (Qi) and unseen (Alonzo). The Acts that were considered included: the Equality Act 2010 with section 6 providing a definition of disability; the Human Rights Act 1998, which gives guidance on working with service users and their families and respecting their human rights; and the Care Act 2014, for example sections 77 and 78, which explain how local authorities should determine who is eligible for support. Also considered was legislation that applies to children and young people, for example, the Local Authority and Social Services Act 1970, section 7, which identifies the local authorities' responsibilities to children who experience D/deafblindness, and the Children Act 1989 with section 1 highlighting the welfare of the child is paramount, section 17 considering children in need such as children with disabilities and section 47 providing guidance for safeguarding children. The 2004 amendment of the Children Act 1989 was also discussed, for example, section 53 taking due consideration of the child's wishes and feelings, as well as the Children and Families Act 2014, especially Part 3 (s19–83), which relates to children and young people with special educational needs and disabilities/impairments.

So once again, before moving on to the next chapter which will consider law specific to adults, the Care Act 2014, we would like to end this chapter by encouraging you to record your personal reflections and individual thoughts; you may like to write them directly in this book to keep for future reference.

END OF CHAPTER ACTIVITY TO CAPTURE PERSONAL REFLECTIONS AND INDIVIDUAL THOUGHTS

Critically reflect on this chapter and what you have learned, recording your own personal thoughts and feelings; as in previous chapters, use the mindmaps to assist you. The reflective model you might like to consider in this chapter is in Figure 9.1 – Maclean's Big 6 reflective model (2020) – in which six aspects of reflection are considered.

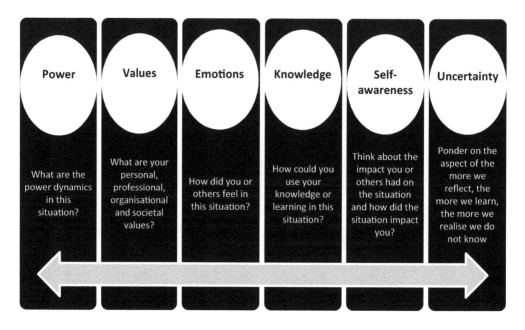

Figure 9.1 Maclean's Big 6 reflective model
Adapted from Maclean (2020)

The Big 6 model can be useful in writing critical analysis and would be a useful tool when writing specific incident reports (Maclean, 2020) such as court reports. Maclean (2020) posits that the Big 6 model can be useful at any stage of reflection, so could be used when first being allocated a case, to handing over or completion of it. Refer back to the case studies of Qi and Alonzo and reflect upon the Big 6 model in the context of the legislation we have considered in this chapter. Also, as in previous chapters, consider if there are any anti-discriminatory or anti-oppressive practice issues (Equality Act 2010) that stand out for you.

Capture your personal reflections and individual thoughts here

REFERENCES

Beckett, A E and Campbell, T (2015) The Social Model of Disability as an Oppositional Device. *Disability & Society*, 30(2): 270–83.

British Deaf Association (2015) What is Deaf Culture? [online] Available at: https://bda.org.uk/what-is-deaf-culture (accessed 4 March 2022).

Care Act 2014 [online] Available at: www.legislation.gov.uk/ukpga/2014/23/contents (accessed 4 March 2022).

Children Act 1989 [online] Available at: www.legislation.gov.uk/ukpga/1989/41/contents (accessed 4 March 2022).

Children Act 2004 Amendment [online] Available at: www.legislation.gov.uk/ukpga/2004/31/contents (accessed 4 March 2022).

Children and Families Act 2014 Part 3 [online] Available at: www.legislation.gov.uk/ukpga/2014/6/part/3 (accessed 4 March 2022).

Department of Health (2014) Care and Support for Deafblind Children and Adults Policy Guidance. [online] Available at: www.gov.uk/government/publications/deafblind-people-guidance-for-local-authorities (accessed 4 March 2022).

Equality Act 2010 [online] Available at: www.legislation.gov.uk/ukpga/2010/15/contents (accessed 4 March 2022).

Evans, H D (2019) 'Trial by Fire': Forms of Impairment Disclosure and Implications for Disability Identity. *Disability & Society*, 34(5): 726–46.

Evans, M (2017) Empowering People Experiencing Usher Syndrome as Participants in Research. *British Journal of Social Work*, 47(8): 2328–45.

Evans, M (2018a) Acting Reasonably: Making 'Reasonable Adjustments' for People with Disabilities. [online] Available at: https://rcni.com/nursing-management/opinion/comment/acting-reasonably-making-reasonable-adjustments-people-disabilities-142861 (accessed 4 March 2022).

Evans, M (2018b) *Usher Syndrome: A Phenomenological Study of Adults Across the Lifespan Living in England*. Published PhD thesis (740172). [online] Available at: https://ethos.bl.uk/OrderDetails.do?did=1&uin=uk.bl.ethos.740172 (accessed 4 March 2022).

Evans, M and Baillie, L (2021) Usher Syndrome, an Unseen Hidden Disability: A Phenomenological Study of Adults Across the Lifespan Living in England. *Disability and Society*. [online] Available at: www.tandfonline.com/eprint/ZZ73HFXHAVQEVNBV8GIA/full?target=10.1080/09687599.2021.1889981 (accessed 4 March 2022).

Evans, M and Whittaker, A (2010) *Sensory Awareness and Social Work*. London: Sage/Learning Matters.

Gov.UK (2010) Definition of Disability Under the Equality Act 2010. [online] Available at: www.gov.uk/definition-of-disability-under-equality-act-2010 (accessed 4 March 2022).

Hardy, R (2018) Social Work with d/Deaf people: Key Issues in Adult Safeguarding. [online] Available at: www.communitycare.co.uk/2018/09/19/social-work-d-deaf-people-key-issues-adult-safeguarding (accessed 4 March 2022).

Hughes, B and Paterson, K (1997) The Social Model of Disability and the Disappearing Body: Towards a Sociology of Impairment. *Disability & Society*, 12(3): 325–40.

Human Rights Act 1998 [online] Available at: www.legislation.gov.uk/ukpga/1998/42/contents (accessed 4 March 2022).

Jenks, A (2019) Crip Theory and the Disabled Identity: Why Disability Politics Needs Impairment. *Disability & Society*, 34(3): 449–69.

Local Authority and Social Services Act 1970 [online] Available at: www.legislation.gov.uk/ukpga/1970/42 (accessed 8 March 2022).

Maclean, S (2020) Big 6 Reflective Model. [online] Available at: www.youtube.com/watch?v=eSCUPKm5PTY (accessed 4 March 2022).

Mencap (2021) Transition into Adult Services. [online] Available at: www.mencap.org.uk/advice-and-support/children-and-young-people/transition-adult-services (accessed 4 March 2022).

Mental Capacity Act 2005 [online] Available at: www.legislation.gov.uk/ukpga/2005/9/contents (accessed 4 March 2022).

Muscular Dystrophy UK (2021) Duchenne Muscular Dystrophy (DMD). [online] Available at: www.musculardystrophyuk.org/conditions/duchenne-muscular-dystrophy-dmd (accessed 4 March 2022).

National Deaf Children's Society (NDCS) (2020) Rights to Equality in England, Scotland and Wales. [online] Available at: www.ndcs.org.uk/information-and-support/your-rights/understanding-your-rights/rights-to-equality-in-england-scotland-and-wales (accessed 4 March 2022).

National Society for the Prevention of Cruelty to Children (NSPCC) (2021) Guidance on Protecting d/Deaf and Disabled Children and Young People from Abuse. [online] Available at: https://learning.nspcc.org.uk/safeguarding-child-protection/deaf-and-disabled-children (accessed 4 March 2022).

Ofori-Ansah, S, Evans, M, Jones, J and Thomas, N (2021) Decision-making Experiences of Young Adults with Kidney Disease and Other Long-term Conditions. *Journal of Renal Care*. https://doi.org/10.1111/jorc.12367

Sense (2020) Deafblind Guidance. [online] Available at: www.sense.org.uk/get-support/information-and-advice/deafblind-guidance (accessed 4 March 2022).

Shakespeare, T (1992) A Response to Liz Crow. *Coalition*, September: 40–2.

Social Work England (2021) Registration. [online] Available at: www.socialworkengland.org.uk/registration (accessed 9 March 2022).

Union of the Physically Impaired Against Segregation (UPIAS) (1976) *Fundamental Principles of Disability*. London: Union of the Physically Impaired Against Segregation (UPIAS).

Williams, P and Evans, M (2013) *Social Work with People with Learning Difficulties*. London: Learning Matters Ltd/Sage.

PART 3 LAW SPECIFIC TO ADULTS

10 Care Act 2014

INTRODUCTION

Having learned about legislation relevant to social work practice with children and adults who experience impairment seen and unseen, this chapter considers social work practice and legislation when working with adults, primarily the Care Act (CA) 2014. There are five parts to the Care Act: Care and Support, Care Standards, Health, Health and Social Care, and General. The main focus in this chapter will be on Part 1, Care and Support, as this is the part that social workers principally need to understand in order to provide best practice to the persons with whom they are working. The six key principles to safeguarding will also be discussed. As in other chapters, the Care Act 2014 will be considered in the context of application to practice.

The Care Act 2014 outlines there is a need to assess any individual who appears to need care and support (SCIE, 2015) whether the individual is likely to be eligible for state-funded care or not; however, consent is required from an individual or their representative (the person authorised under the Mental Capacity Act 2005) if the person is deemed to lack capacity before they can be assessed (SCIE, 2014).

The reason for focusing on the Care Act 2014 is because social workers are an integral part of social care provision and work with the most vulnerable adults in society, for example people who experience disability (CA, s77; also see Chapter 9) ranging from temporary disabilities, such as a broken leg, to permanent disabilities, such as leg amputation, as well as safeguarding risk (s42) which could incorporate physical abuse, including neglect of medication. Experiences of domestic violence are another aspect, which takes in honour-based violence and sexual abuse, the latter of which takes account of involvement in pornography. Psychological abuse, which also comprises unreasonable withdrawal of services or support, is included, together with financial abuse, which consists of coercion, as well as theft or fraud and modern slavery (exploitation of individuals for profitable or personal gain – see also Modern Slavery Act 2015).

Individuals also experience various forms of discriminatory behaviour where people may be treated unfairly because of their age, gender, race or disability (see Equality Act 2010) as well as organisational or individual abuse or neglect. People also experience acts of omission, especially in providing medical needs, and self-neglect, including hoarding (keeping lots of items regardless of their value), poverty and advancing age, which can contribute to a plethora of conditions such as dementia (see Chapter 6). Thus, supporting people to live well becomes more complex in contemporary society.

The chapter is important because social workers need to conduct assessments (s9) but, as highlighted above, also understand that service provision cannot be imposed on people unless they lack capacity (see Chapter 6) and it is in the person's best interests. Social workers also need to provide care plans (s25), review services (s27) and understand what happens when a person is unable to live in their own home (s39), as well as the concept of how the local authority imposes charges (s14, s16) and the power the local authority has for recovering charges (s69, s70). Overall, it is central for social workers to have knowledge and understanding of the Care Act 2014 to enable them to practise competently and efficiently in order to support and empower the people with whom they are working.

Next the case study of Kobi will be considered in the context of the Care Act 2014.

Case study

Kobi is a 35 year-old Black British male; Kobi's parents came to the UK from Ghana. Kobi's Ghanaian heritage is important to him, as is his love of cooking Ghanaian food, for example jollof (rice dish), banku (fermented corn and cassava dough) and plantain with egg stew. Kobi was living life to the full; he was successful in his career, lived in a beautiful apartment in the centre of the city, drove a prestigious car and enjoyed socialising. One day, Kobi collapses while on a business trip in the UK and is rushed to hospital, where he is diagnosed with a rare heart condition and Kobi's life changes in an instant. Kobi is now very unwell and he can no longer drive or work, which places him in financial difficulty.

What needs to be ascertained is whether Kobi is entitled to support under the Care Act 2014; does Kobi fulfil the eligibility criteria (s13), will Kobi's diversity and quality in provision of service be promoted (s6), will Kobi be entitled to an assessment (s9) and will he be provided with information and advice (s4) to meet his needs? In this chapter, you will be provided with knowledge and guidance to enable you to apply the Care Act 2014 in practice.

FIVE PARTS OF THE CARE ACT 2014

As highlighted previously, there are five parts to the Act (Care and Support, Care Standards, Health, Health and Social Care, and General) and while each of these parts will be referred to, Part 1: Care and Support will receive principal attention because social workers need to understand care and support legislation to underpin their practice.

Part 1: Care and Support

Part 1 of the Act covers sections 1–80. As you can imagine, it is not possible to cover every section in this one chapter, but the weblink for the Care Act 2014 is in the reference list for you to further explore sections you may think will be useful to you in your practice.

General responsibilities of the local authority

Under the Care Act sections 1–7, the local authority has responsibilities, including promoting an individual's well-being (s1), preventing needs for care and support (s2), promoting integration of care and support with, for example health services (s3), providing information and advice (s4), promoting diversity and quality of provision of services (s5), co-operating generally (s6) and co-operating in specific cases (s7).

So let us return to the case study of Kobi. The social worker would become involved once a referral has been made; in Kobi's case, the referral would most likely have been made by the hospital. The next step would be for the social worker to contact Kobi to conduct an assessment of need (s9). The social worker's role is to consider if under the Care Act 2014 Kobi meets the eligibility criteria (s13) and if he is entitled to support. The social worker is also required to promote and respect Kobi's cultural heritage and diversity (s6).

Section 1 stipulates that the well-being of the individual is promoted; what do you think that means in practice? Well, consider what is meant by promoting well-being; it denotes that action is required, so actively seeking to promote well-being. It may be that Kobi feels disempowered and does not want to talk about his situation; he may not have come to terms with it himself. However, you could leave Kobi information and advice (s4) so that if he wants to consider options when he is alone or at a later date, he has the information to hand to be able to consider his options.

Section 2 considers preventing needs for care and support, which means that the local authority needs to provide or arrange for services and support to prevent or delay development in an area that an individual needs for care and support; this section applies this principle to carers if there any as well, so as to prevent or delay the development by carers with regard to needs for support. However, the regulations may allow the local authority to make charges for providing services, so, in Kobi's case although he may be eligible for services and support, depending on his financial status, he may be required to fund services partly or wholly himself.

Section 3, as highlighted above, considers promoting integration of care and support with, for example, health services. Under this section, care and support provision refers to provision to meet the individual's needs for care and support; provision to meet the carer's needs for support; and provision of services, facilities, resources or other actions that can influence needs for care and support.

Assessing needs

This part of the Act covers sections 9–13 and is key to social work practice because it considers assessment of an individual's needs for care and support (s9), assessment of a carer's needs for support (s10) and the eligibility criteria (s13). If, as in Kobi's case, an individual requires an assessment of need for care and support (s9), the local authority must assess whether the adult does have needs for care and support and, if he/she does have needs, what those needs are. To be eligible for services (s13), a person would have to be assessed as being unable to meet two or more outcomes specified in the regulations, for example caring for nutritional needs, toilet needs, personal hygiene, wearing appropriate clothing, maintaining a liveable home environment, developing and maintaining personal and family relationships, accessing and participating in work, education or volunteering, using facilities in the local community (for example, public transport) and caring for a child (SCIE, 2014).

There are certain conditions that must be met to meet the eligibility criteria, including the following.

1. The individual's needs for care and support arise from or are related to a physical or mental impairment or illness and are not caused by other circumstantial factors.

2. As a result of the individual's needs, the person is unable to achieve two or more of the outcomes specified in the regulations (as described above).

3. As a result of being unable to achieve these outcomes, there is, or there is likely to be, a significant effect on the individual's well-being.

(SCIE, 2014)

As Kobi's case study highlighted, he can no longer work or drive a car, due to his heart condition; additionally, he is too weak to use public transport. Therefore, he is unable to meet two outcomes and would meet the eligibility criteria (s13).

Carers too have to meet certain conditions.

1. The carer's needs for support arise because they are providing necessary care to an individual.

2. As a result of their caring responsibilities, the carer's physical or mental health either is deteriorating or is at risk of doing so or the carer is unable to accomplish the outcomes as specified in the regulations (as highlighted above).

3. As a result of being unable to attain these outcomes, there is, or there is likely to be, a significant impact on the carer's well-being (SCIE, 2014). However, something to be noted is that the Care Act 2014 for the first time gave carers rights and recognition.

Charging and assessing financial resources

This part of the Act covers sections 14–17. Section 14 outlines that the local authority has the power to make charges under sections 18–20. Where the local authority has conducted a financial assessment and deemed that charges are relevant, they would charge the individual under section 14. In the case of Kobi, as highlighted in the case study, his sudden change in work-related circumstances has resulted in financial difficulties; therefore, in Kobi's case as he is below the financial limit he may not be charged for care and support. However, should Kobi's circumstances change and he becomes financially solvent then, as highlighted, the local authority can charge if they provide care and support.

Duties and powers to meet needs

Sections 18–23 of the Act include the duty of the local authority to meet needs for care and support (s18), the power of the local authority to meet needs for care and support (s19), the duty and power of the local authority to meet carers' needs for care and support (s20) and exceptions for individuals subject to immigration control (s21).

Next steps after assessment

Sections 24–30 are key to social work practice because they explain the steps for the local authority to take after an assessment has been conducted (s24), the importance of care and support plans (s25), information and advice about personal budgets (s26), review of the care and support plan (s27) and independent personal budgets (s28). The care and support plan (s27) is prepared by the local authority but must also involve the individual themselves and the carer if relevant and outlines the needs for care and support for an individual. The care plan is reviewed by the local authority to ensure the care plan still meets the individual's needs for care and support; it may involve a reviewed assessment (s9) of the individual's care and support needs, a reviewed carer's assessment (s10) if relevant and a financial assessment. Where needs are met by direct payments (s31–s33), the care plan must specify the amount and frequency of the direct payment; this will be discussed a little further in the next section.

An independent personal budget (s28) outlines what the cost of the care and support needs of an individual would be for the local authority the person is associated with. The personal budget can be reviewed by the local authority and the person receiving the budget can ask for it to be reviewed; the social worker working with Kobi may wish to discuss this with him.

Direct payments

Sections 31–33 cover adults with capacity to request direct payments (s31), adults without capacity to request direct payments (s32) and direct payment further provision (s33). So to clarify, the personal budget (s28) is a statement of the cost the local authority will pay for an individual's care and support needs and direct payments are where the personal budget specified is wholly or partly paid to the individual or nominated person (s31, s33). Where an individual lacks capacity, section 32 outlines that an authorised person can make requests for direct payments, for example if a person is authorised under the Mental Capacity Act 2005 (Chapter 6), to make decisions for a person. Section 33 also explains about conditions local authorities may attach to making direct payments and cases where the local authority must review direct payments currently being made. Think about Kobi: his life has changed drastically and he may feel disempowered, so direct payments may empower him to have more control over his life.

Continuity of care and support when an adult moves

Sections 37 and 38 identify measures to be taken should an individual move out of accommodation or into accommodation, into the community or into their own home.

Establishing where a person lives

Establishing where a person lives is covered in sections 39–41 and includes where a person's ordinary residence is (s39), so this would mean where a person lived prior to needing care and support. This is important because who funds care and support needs will depend on where a person lived and their financial status. Section 40 outlines how to approach disputes about ordinary residence or continuity of care (where a person needs ongoing care and support) and section 41 considers financial adjustments between local authorities.

Safeguarding adults at risk of abuse or neglect

Sections 42–47 refer to safeguarding and therefore are of importance to social work; these sections cover enquiry by the local authority (s42) should an alert be raised, Safeguarding Adult Boards (SABs, s43), which each local authority should establish to help and protect individuals in their area, safeguarding adult reviews (s44) to ensure individuals are kept safe, especially if the adult dies and the SAB suspects the death resulted from abuse or neglect, supply of information (s45), abolition of local authorities' power to remove persons in need of care (s46) and protecting the property of persons being cared for away from home (s47).

Going back to the case study of Kobi and applying section 47 of the Care Act to practice; the situation is now that Kobi has moved from his concierge-supported city apartment and is currently living in a hostel waiting to be re-housed. Kobi's health is still deteriorating as he is on the waiting list for a heart transplant and has become unwell and had to go into hospital for a medical procedure. Kobi still has his possessions from his previous apartment; while he is away from home, the local authority has a duty to prevent or mitigate the loss or damage of his property (s47).

Sections 48–52 focus on provider failure and explore temporary duties on local authorities and cross-border cases (eg Wales and Ireland), while sections 53–67 on market oversight include informing local authorities of care provider concerns (s56).

Transition from children to adult care and support

This section of the Act covers sections 58 to 66 and includes assessment of a child's needs for care and support (s58), assessment of the child's carers' needs for care and support (s60) and assessment of young carers' needs for support (s63). As previously considered in Chapter 6, it is crucial for social workers to understand transitioning legislation because there should be no gap in support (Mencap, 2021) to ensure children and their families/carers are supported and their well-being promoted (s1–s6).

Independent advocacy support

Local authorities have a duty to involve people in their care and support. Regardless of the complexities a person experiences, the local authority still has a duty to assist people to express their wishes and feelings (Human Rights Act 1998; Equality Act 2010; SCIE, 2021a). An Independent Care Act Advocate (ICAA) is similar to an Independent Mental Capacity Advocate (IMCA, see Chapter 6) but is appointed under the Care Act 2014. Although referred by a social worker or other person, the ICAA is independent of the local authority and is there to support the individual to enable them to present their thoughts, feelings and views and maximise their range of involvement in their care and support needs (SCIE, 2021a). The ICAA is involved in assessments, plans and reviews (s67) as well as safeguarding enquiries and reviews (s68). Kobi was offered an ICAA but declined, and his views were respected.

Sections 69 and 70 outline enforcement of debts, such as recovery of charges (s69). Section 71 focuses on the review of funding provision, for example the five yearly review by the Secretary of State, while section 72 deals with appeals, for example decisions taken by the local authority.

Areas covered in the miscellaneous sections (s73–s79) include discharge of hospital patients for care and support needs (s74), aftercare under the Mental Health Act 1983 (s75), prisoners and persons in approved premises (s76) and registers of sight-impaired adults and disabled adults (s77), which is considered in greater detail in Chapter 9.

General interpretation

Interpretation (s80) is presented in table form and is useful because it provides a description, for example abuse, and then provides the section this is covered under, such as section 42(3).

Having considered Part 1 in some detail, Parts 2 to 5 will be briefly explained. You are encouraged to look at these parts in more detail as part of your personal study.

Part 2: Care Standards

Part 2 of the Act covers sections 81–95, which include quality of services, the Care Quality Commission, increasing the independence of the Care Quality Commission and false or misleading information.

Part 3: Health

Part 3 of the Act covers sections 96–120 and covers establishment of Health Education England, national functions of Health Education England, local functions of Health Education England, establishment of the Health Research Authority and the Health Research Authority's policy on research ethics committees.

Part 4: Health and Social Care

Part 4 of the Act covers sections 121 and 122, which include the integration fund – integration of care and support with health services.

Part 5: General

Part 5 of the Act incorporates sections 123 to 129 and covers general interpretation, for example, that the financial year means a period of 12 months ending with the 31 March and that the health service means the comprehensive health service in England.

Having considered the five parts of the Act, next the six key principles in safeguarding will be deliberated.

SIX KEY PRINCIPLES IN SAFEGUARDING

There are six key principles in safeguarding, empowerment, protection, prevention, proportionality, partnership and accountability, which apply to all health and care settings (SCIE, 2021b). Although these principles were introduced originally by the Department of Health (2011) to provide guidance for the role of health service practitioners with regard to providing best practice when safeguarding adults, when the Care Act came into effect they were embedded into the Act (SCIE, 2021b).

Principle 1: Empowerment

There is the presumption that decisions and consent will be person led so that adults are in control of their care. If actions are taken without consent, then clear justification needs to be provided and the person needs to be included in the decision-making process as far as possible. All decisions made must respect the individual's culture, beliefs, age and lifestyle. So for example, when working with Kobi, you would need to ensure that his Ghanaian heritage is respected as it is important to him. This principle also links with section 5 of the Care Act (CA), which stipulates that local authorities are required to promote diversity and quality in provision of services, including having a variety of providers to choose from should care and support be needed (CA, s6), having sufficient information to make an informed decision and having best interests and promotion of well-being (CA, s1) central for not only the service user but also carers.

Principle 2: Protection

Support and representation are to be provided for those persons in the greatest need; this includes supporting individuals to protect themselves. Again, when working with Kobi it would be important to ensure he has support and representation, especially at a time when he may feel disempowered by his recent diagnosis.

Principle 3: Prevention

Prevention of harm and/or abuse is essential; this also includes supporting individuals to reduce risk and/or harm that are unacceptable to them, as well as decreasing risks of neglect or abuse arising within health services.

Principle 4: Proportionality

Proportionality considers the least intrusive reaction to risk that arises; therefore, reaction to risk should consider the nature and gravity of the concern while managing the situation in the most effective manner. Reaction must be conducted in the least restrictive way and again take into account the individual's culture, belief, age, wishes and lifestyle (CA, s6).

Principle 5: Partnerships

This principle focuses on partnership working, resolving through collaborative working to avert, detect and respond to harm and/or abuse. It may be that when working with Kobi, as he has a heart defect, you will also be working with clinical/medical professionals as well as occupational therapy (OT) and later possibly rehabilitation services. As all services focus on particular areas of need, collaborative working would result in Kobi receiving a person-centred service.

Principle 6: Accountability

Accountability and transparency when delivering safeguarding services is essential, which includes accountability to patients, the general public and governing bodies (a group of people who develop policies and direct affairs, for example, local government) and partner agencies (working together to safeguard).

Having considered the six key principles in safeguarding and its application to the case study of Kobi, next the duties and responsibilities of the social worker will be reflected upon.

DUTIES AND RESPONSIBILITIES OF THE SOCIAL WORKER

Social workers need to understand the Care Act 2014 to provide care and support services to vulnerable people. Social workers have a duty to promote diversity (s5) and contribute towards inclusion and as far as possible ensure quality of service provision. As highlighted in Chapter 6, social workers not only have a duty to work within the law but also work within Social Work England's professional standards, which includes promoting the rights, strengths and well-being (s1) of people, families and communities, as well as being accountable (see six principles in safeguarding) for the quality of practice and decisions they make.

THE CARE ACT 2014 – BRIEF SUMMARY

○   Where individuals are in need of care and support, the local authority has a responsibility to promote an individual's well-being (s1) and provide an assessment (s9), whether the individual is likely to be eligible for state-funded care or not.

○   Consent is required from an individual before they are assessed.

○   The six key principles in safeguarding are empowerment, protection, prevention, proportionality, partnership and accountability.

○   There are five parts to the Act: Care and Support, Care Standards, Health, Health and Social Care, and General.

○   Social workers often use Part 1 of the Care Act 2014 with the following sections used in practice: s1 promoting an individual's well-being, s4 providing information and advice, s5 promoting diversity and quality of provision of service, s9 assessment, s10 carer's assessment, s13 eligibility criteria, s25 care plans, s27 reviews, s33 direct payments, s42–s47 safeguarding and s58 assessment of child's needs for adult care and support (transitioning).

○   An Independent Care Act Advocate (ICAA) is referred by a social worker or other person to support the person to enable them to present their thoughts, feelings and views and maximise their range of involvement in their care and support needs.

DECISIONS MADE ON THE CASE STUDY

To enable you to see how the decision was made see below.

The case study relating to Kobi

As outlined in the case study, Kobi's life had changed suddenly, which is often the case in practice. Kobi gave consent for the assessment (s9) as he realised he needed support due to his health condition. The social worker allocated to Kobi promoted his well-being (s1), provided information and advice (s4), respected Kobi's Ghanaian heritage (s5) and, once a care plan (s25) had been completed, ensured a review (s27) was conducted to promote best practice. Also when Kobi was admitted to hospital, protection of his possessions was taken into account (s47).

Key points to remember

The Care Act 2014's framework indicates that there is a need to assess individuals who present as needing care and support, whether the individual is likely to be eligible for state-funded care or not. However, it is important to note that consent is required from an individual before they are assessed. As with other legislation, if you as a social worker are not familiar with the Care Act you will not be able to apply it in practice. While it does not mean you need to know every section from memory, you do need to ensure you have a solid foundation of understanding which you can build upon, depending on the needs of the people with whom you are working. Knowledge and understanding are important to apply the law in practice.

TEST YOUR LEGISLATIVE KNOWLEDGE

Answers are at the back of the book.

Questions

- What is the purpose of the Care Act 2014?

- How many parts are there to the Care Act 2014 and what are they?

- Which part of the Care Act 2014 would you likely use the most in your social work role?

- Which sections of Part 1 of the Care Act 2014 would you be most likely to use in your role as a social worker?

- What are the six key principles in safeguarding?

- What is an Independent Care Act Advocate (ICAA)?

CHAPTER SUMMARY

In summary, this chapter explored the Care Act 2014 and its application to practice by considering the case study of Kobi and applying legislation to it. Elements of the Care Act that were discussed in this chapter incorporated the five parts to the Act: Care and Support, Care Standards, Health, Health and Social Care, and General. Sections of the Act that social workers need to understand for best practice include s1 promoting an individual's well-being, s4 providing information and advice, s5 promoting diversity and quality of provision of service, s9 assessment, s10 carer's assessment, s13 eligibility criteria, s25 care plans, s27 reviews, s33 direct payments, safeguarding s42–s47, s58 assessment of child's needs for adult care and support (transitioning), which are all contained in Part 1 of the Act. The six key principles in safeguarding were outlined: empowerment, protection, prevention, proportionality, partnership and accountability, as well as the importance of the Independent Care Act Advocate (ICAA). However, as highlighted at the beginning of the chapter, the Care Act is an extensive piece of legislation and we were not able to cover every aspect of it in this chapter. You are encouraged to explore all the parts independently to practise effectively and provide individual tailormade support to the people with whom you work. So before moving on to the next chapter on practice-related study skills, once again we would like to end this chapter by encouraging you to record your personal reflections and individual thoughts; you may like to write them directly in this book to keep for future reference.

Establishing where a person lives (**s39–s41**), **s39** where a person's ordinary residence is

s41 adjustments between local authorities

Safeguarding adults at risk of abuse or neglect (**s42–s47**), **s42** enquiry by local authority

s43 Safeguarding Adult Boards

s47 protecting property of adults being cared for away from home

s5 promoting diversity and quality in provision of service

Meeting needs for care, **s8** how to meet needs for care

Direct payments (**s31–s33**), **s31** adults with capacity to require direct payments

s32 adults without capacity to request direct payments

Local authority responsibilities (**s1–s6**), **s1** promoting individuals' well-being

s2 preventing needs for care and support

s3 promoting integration of care and support with health services

s4 providing information and advice

Care Act 2014: Part 1 Care and Support

Assessing needs (**s9–s13**), **s9** assessment of adult needs for care and support

s10 assessment of a carer's needs for care and support

s13 eligibility criteria

Charging and assessing financial resources (**s14–s17**), **s14** power of local authority to charge

s17 assessment of financial resources

Duties and power to meet needs (**s18–s23**), **s18** duty to meet needs for care and support

Next steps after assessment (**s24–s30**), **s24** the steps for the local authority to take and **s26** personal budget

Transition for children to adult care and support (**s58–s66**), **s58** assessment of child's needs for adult care and support

END OF CHAPTER ACTIVITY TO CAPTURE PERSONAL REFLECTIONS AND INDIVIDUAL THOUGHTS

Critically reflect on this chapter and what you have learned, recording your own personal thoughts and feelings; as in previous chapters, use the mindmap to assist you. The reflective model you might like to consider in this chapter is Gibbs' six-stage reflective cycle (Gibbs, 1988). The stages are: description, for example what was the experience? Feelings, what were your thoughts and feelings? Evaluation, what did you think was good or bad about what you experienced? Analysis, what was your analysis of the situation? Conclusion, was there anything else you think you could have done? Action plan, if the experience came up again, what would you do differently? (Gibbs, 1988). Gibbs posits that we learn from our experiences and the cyclical structure of the model not only provides organisation with regard to the reflective process but also highlights that experiences are often repeated. This is often the case in social work practice because although experiences will not be exactly the same, assessments (s9, s10), care plans (s25) and reviews (s27) will be repeated experiences.

When you go to a panel to request services for the people with whom you are working, sometimes you will not be able to achieve the results you wanted due to limited resources; thus, although you have to be realistic, this is where the law can support you in practice. Knowing, understanding and applying the law can strengthen your application. Also being reflective before and after going to the panel can provide the potential for you to consider what challenges could be raised, what happened, what you did and what you could do differently next time. Critically reflect on the case study of Kobi in the context of the Care Act 2014; how would you apply the Care Act in practice when working with Kobi? Also, as in previous chapters, deliberate upon whether there are any anti-discriminatory or any anti-oppressive practice issues (Equality Act 2010) that stand out for you.

Capture your personal reflections and individual thoughts here

REFERENCES

Care Act 2014 [online] Available at: www.legislation.gov.uk/ukpga/2014/23/contents/enacted (accessed 4 March 2022).

Department of Health (2011) *Safeguarding Adults: The Role of Health Service Practitioners*. [online] Available at: https://assets.publishing.service.gov.uk/government/uploads/system/uploads/attachment_data/file/215714/dh_125233.pdf (accessed 4 March 2022).

Equality Act 2010 [online] Available at: www.legislation.gov.uk/ukpga/2010/15/contents (accessed 4 March 2022).

Gibbs, G (1988) *Learning by Doing: A Guide to Teaching and Learning Methods. Further Education Unit*. Oxford: Oxford Polytechnic.

Human Rights Act 1998 [online] Available at: www.legislation.gov.uk/ukpga/1998/42/contents (accessed 4 March 2022).

Mencap (2021) Transition into Adult Services. [online] Available at: www.mencap.org.uk/advice-and-support/children-and-young-people/transition-adult-services (accessed 4 March 2022).

Mental Capacity Act 2005 [online] Available at: www.legislation.gov.uk/ukpga/2005/9/contents (accessed 4 March 2022).

Modern Slavery Act 2015 [online] Available at: www.gov.uk/government/collections/modern-slavery-bill (accessed 9 March 2022).

Social Care Institute for Excellence (SCIE) (2014) Eligibility under the Care Act 2014. [online] Available at: www.scie.org.uk/care-act-2014/assessment-and-eligibility/eligibility/criteria (accessed 4 March 2022).

Social Care Institute for Excellence (SCIE) (2015) Care Act Guidance on Strengths-based Approaches. [online] Available at: www.scie.org.uk/strengths-based-approaches/guidance (accessed 4 March 2022).

Social Care Institute for Excellence (SCIE) (2021a) Commissioning Independent Advocacy. [online] Available at: www.scie.org.uk/advocacy/commissioning/duties#under-the-act (accessed 4 March 2022).

Social Care Institute for Excellence (SCIE) (2021b) What are the Six Key Principles of Safeguarding? [online] Available at: www.scie.org.uk/safeguarding/adults/introduction/six-principles (accessed 4 March 2022).

PART 4 PRACTICE-RELATED STUDY SKILLS

Applying the law to social work practice

INTRODUCTION

It is all very well teaching you the law and knowledge, but you also need the confidence to apply that knowledge of the law in practice. This chapter provides an opportunity for you to pause for thought and to think about applying the law to case studies, and perhaps consider decisions made on the case studies in previous chapters. Also, you could create your own mindmaps or expand on the examples provided, as well as reflecting upon key points to remember and reviewing testing your legislative knowledge. Finally, ponder on your responses to activities, capture your personal reflections and individual thoughts and consider what anti-discriminatory practice and/or anti-oppressive practice issues stood out for you.

To avoid over-complicating the law and encourage your concentration, in this chapter particular focus will be given to the Children Act 1989/2004, Care Act 2014, Mental Capacity Act 2005/2019 and Mental Health Act 1983/2007. The intention is for you to learn techniques to apply the law, so, for example, in training or early practice you may not have worked with trafficked children, but because you have developed techniques to apply the law, you will be able to utilise those techniques to apply the law in any practice situation you may find yourself in. Thus, this book will be useful not only in academic settings but also on placement and post qualifying.

With regard to practice-related study skills support, this chapter will focus on three areas:

o   preparation to undertake a social work law exam;

o   essay preparation;

o   applying the law on placement.

However, it is not just about passing an exam or writing an essay but also about building social work confidence, understanding the law, applying the law and developing professional judgement as you enter practice. Next the first area of practice-related study skills support, exam preparation, will be considered.

UNDERTAKING A SOCIAL WORK LAW EXAM

Below you can see what an exam may look like. Remember that each institution will have their own strategy/structure for conducting the exam and you will need to refer to your own institution for clear guidance; this is an example only.

> ## *Our note to you*
>
> When you are preparing for your exam, refer to the mindmaps you have been using; remember which colour refers to which Act of Parliament to prompt you. Refer back to the key points indicated in each chapter and reflect upon your personal reflections and individual thoughts.

Exam question example

This section provides guidance of how you would apply the following legislation to an exam:

○ Children Act 1989/2004;

○ Care Act 2014;

○ Mental Health Act 1983/2007;

○ Mental Capacity Act 2005/2019.

Start of example exam paper

Instructions to students

Answer ALL questions. There are four questions in total. Your marks will be weighted evenly across all the questions.

Read the case studies and answer the questions that follow, explaining the legislative framework relevant to the case study. You are expected to evidence knowledge and understanding of the law. You are also expected to demonstrate the link between legislation and social work practice, explaining how and why the law should be applied in each practice scenario.

Please note you are not being asked to write about ideas for services or support that may assist or resolve this situation. You are being asked to discuss in what way the law might apply to this case study.

Students are permitted to bring in and consult an unmarked copy of:

Evans, M and Harvey, D (2022) *Social Work Law: Using the Law in Practice*. St Albans: Critical Publishing.

Case study 1

Sarah and Tim are twins, aged six, with mild–moderate learning disabilities; both are on the autistic spectrum. Sarah told her teacher, Miss Okuntunde, that their mum and dad are constantly telling them they are bad, useless and stupid and they had better hope that their mum and dad live a very long time because no-one else will want them. While talking to Sarah, Miss Okuntunde notices quite bad bruising to Sarah's legs. When Sarah is asked about them, she tells Miss Okuntunde that she and Tim are really badly behaved, and their parents hit them to make them be good. Miss Okuntunde asked to see Sarah and Tim's parents, and, after talking to them, it emerged that their parents are really struggling with the children's behaviour and often deem it appropriate to discipline the children; when questioned on the severity of the discipline, both parents become angry and aggressive and walk out of the school. The school has referred the case to social services.

Drawing on your understanding and knowledge of the Children Act 1989/2004, describe how you would approach this case study if you were the social worker.

Case study 2

Gordon is 67 years of age and was diagnosed with Alzheimer's disease a year ago. At first the condition seemed almost non-existent, but over the last few months Gordon's condition seems to have deteriorated rapidly. Gordon's wife of five years, Blessing, is finding it difficult to cope because she says that Gordon is going out in the middle of the night, naked, getting disorientated and often lost; on the last occasion the police found Gordon wandering the streets, wearing just a pair of socks, and brought him home after discovering an SOS band on his wrist that Blessing had insisted he wear to be on the safe side.

Drawing on your knowledge of the Mental Capacity Act 2005/2019, as a social worker what principles would you apply? How would you determine if Gordon lacks capacity? Explain the purpose of a best interests meeting and consider if this would be appropriate in Gordon's situation.

Case study 3

Pierre, aged 40 years, has been in hospital and rehabilitation for a year and a half following a hit and run accident in which he was left paralysed from the waist downwards and is no longer able to work. Prior to the accident, Pierre ran his own successful building business and was a keen rock climber, a hobby he shared with his wife Xia; they have no children or other responsibilities and most weekends were spent enjoying their hobby. Since the accident, Xia has distanced herself from Pierre, saying that although she cares for him, she cannot see herself married to someone who cannot share the interests and hobbies that she has. As Pierre is about to return home, Xia has decided that she cannot care for Pierre and is going to contact a solicitor to file for divorce. Pierre has no siblings and both parents are deceased. Pierre's friends also find it hard to talk to him since the accident as they say that Pierre is different and even self-neglecting. Pierre tells you he feels lonely and has become low and depressed.

Explain how the Care Act 2014 might apply in this case study, including how Pierre's needs for care and support could meet the eligibility criteria threshold.

Case study 4

Greta is a social worker and an Approved Mental Health Professional (AMHP) on duty in the adults with mental health team and has been contacted by the police safeguarding liaison officer and asked to attend an address. Present at the address is a 23 year-old man named Aayansh, who has attempted to jump from his flat on the third floor. After talking to his mother, Amayra, Greta finds that Aayansh has been expressing bizarre beliefs over the past three weeks. For example, he has stated that his mother has been replaced by a robot. He has also stopped eating as he claims that there are people in his food.

Explain the role of the Approved Mental Health Professional and then explain how you would use the Mental Health Act 1983/2007 in practice to support and safeguard Aayansh.

End of example exam paper

Test your knowledge

You have been provided with four case studies pertaining to the Children Act 1989/2004, the Mental Capacity Act 2005, the Care Act 2014 and the Mental Health Act 1983/2007. Before looking at possible responses to the exam paper, try to complete it yourself and then compare your responses to those included in this book. You may want to try again after reviewing the possible responses to see if you can improve your application of law to the case study; the first attempt could be likened to the mock exam and the next attempt like the actual exam paper.

POSSIBLE RESPONSES TO EXAM PAPER

Case study 1: Sarah and Tim, six year-old twins (refer to the case study as outlined earlier for full details)

Question: Drawing on your understanding and knowledge of the Children Act 1989/ 2004, describe how you would approach this case study if you were the social worker.

Possible response

Sarah and Tim are under 18 years of age and would be supported by the Children Act 1989/2004. The Children Act section 1 states that the welfare of the child is paramount (Evans and Harvey, 2022) and as such the local authority has a duty of care towards the children following Miss Okuntunde's referral to social services.

Section 17 of the Children Act 1989 would classify the children as children in need because they have mild–moderate learning disabilities. An amendment to the Children Act in 2004 placed duties on the local authority to support children up to a maximum age of 25 years if the children were to become looked after by the local authority before they were 16 years old (Children Act 2004, s9). Therefore, if Sarah and Tim were to become looked after before the age of 16, they could receive child-centred local authority support up to the age of 25 years. Under the 2004 amendment to the Children Act 1989, Sarah's and Tim's wishes and feelings (s53) would need to be considered as well as the impact their home life may have on their educational achievement (s52).

Returning to the Children Act 1989, as Sarah has bruising on her legs this could indicate risk of physical abuse and provides reasonable cause to suspect that Sarah and Tim are suffering, or are likely to suffer, significant harm (s47), which places a duty on the local authority to investigate. Such investigation would require allocating a social worker to the case to conduct an assessment (Evans and Harvey, 2022).

The social worker would need to speak to Sarah and Tim at school and also conduct a home visit. On the way to the visit, the social worker may be considering various options depending on the situation, for example if Sarah and Tim are at risk of significant harm (s47) and needed to be accommodated, it would be better if Sarah and Tim's parents agreed to voluntary accommodation (s20) as this would lessen anxiety for the children (Evans and Harvey, 2022). However, if Sarah and Tim were at risk of significant harm (s47) and their parents did not engage, in order for the children to be safeguarded, they may be accommodated under an interim care order (s38) or full care order (s31) contingent on the individual situation.

If the situation worsened, the parents were not engaging and Sarah and Tim were considered to be at immediate risk of significant harm (s47), an emergency protection order (EPO, s44) may be applied for; this may also require support from the police (s46).

However, if after conducting an assessment, Sarah and Tim's parents do engage because they recognise they need support with the children's behaviour and the way they deal with it, Sarah, Tim and their parents may be supported (s17).

REFERENCES

Great Britain. Children Act 1989/2004. London: HMSO.

Evans, M and Harvey, D (2022) *Social Work Law: Using the Law in Practice*. St Albans: Critical Publishing.

Our note to you

- Read the question carefully and ensure you answer the question.

- Ensure you relate your response to the legislation you are being asked to discuss; do not digress. You will not gain marks for talking about other legislation. Time should be spent focusing on what you have been asked to discuss.

- This response example demonstrates how both the Children Act 1989 and the 2004 amendment were considered, and responses clearly indicated whether it was the 1989 or the 2004 Act that was being discussed.

- If you are referring to the Children Act 1989 and then change to discussing the 2004 amendment, if you then return back to the Children Act 1989 make it clear to the reader you are doing this.

- Although not every section of the Children Act 1989/2004 has been covered, the sections that were discussed were applied to the case study, indicating legislative knowledge and application to practice.

- Reference was made to the book that was allowed be used in the exam (Evans and Harvey, 2022) in the body of the exam response.

○   A reference list was provided at the end; textbook and legislation were provided.

○   If you are undertaking a handwritten exam, ensure your writing is legible; if the marker cannot read the text, then this will affect your mark.

○   As far as possible, check spelling, grammar and overall presentation.

○   If you are undertaking an exam using a computer, then ensure you double space, use a consistent font style and size (usually Arial, 12 pt) and that the text is black.

Case study 2: Gordon, a 67 year-old man (refer to the case study as outlined earlier for full details)

Question: Drawing on your knowledge of the Mental Capacity Act 2005/2019, as a social worker what principles would you apply? How would you determine if Gordon lacks capacity? Explain the purpose of a best interests meeting and consider if this would be appropriate in Gordon's situation.

Possible response

The Mental Capacity Act (MCA) 2005 applies to all people aged 16 years and over who may lack capacity (s2(1)) as in the case study of Gordon. The MCA provides the legal framework to assess if individuals can make decisions for themselves or if they lack capacity to engender a plan of action to act in the person's best interests (s1, Principle 1, s4); therefore, this Act could support Gordon. There are three parts to the MCA, Part 1 being the part that covers people who lack capacity (s1–s62); incorporated in Part 1 are the five principles (s1), the two-stage test (s2, s3), best interests (s1 principle 4, s4) and Mental Capacity Advocates (s35–s41). Part 2 includes the Court of Protection (s45–s63) and Part 3 incorporates covering the scope of the Act (s62). Part 1 would be the part that would primarily support Gordon.

There are five principles (s1) under the terms of the MCA which would provide the framework for promoting Gordon's best interests (s1, Principle 4, s4) and for making a decision regarding whether Gordon lacks capacity or not (Evans and Harvey, 2022). Principle 1 assumes capacity unless it is established the person does not have capacity. Although initially Gordon is assumed to have capacity, since he is going out in the middle of the night, naked, getting disorientated and often lost, this would mean his behaviour indicates otherwise; therefore, a two-stage test would need to be undertaken to establish if he does or does not have capacity (s2, s3). Principle 2 highlights that a person is not to be treated as unable to make a decision unless all practical steps have been taken without success; therefore, Gordon would be supported and encouraged to engage meaningfully in decision making – Blessing would be valuable in this as she knows him well. Principle 3 posits that a person is not to be treated as unable to make a decision merely because they make an unwise decision. Although some decisions such as buying a garment two sizes too small could be considered to be an unwise decision (Evans and Harvey, 2022), Gordon going out in the middle of the night naked would be an unwise decision as it contributes to his vulnerabilities and may put his personal safety in jeopardy. Principle 4 looks at best interests and the fact that it cannot be determined on the grounds of age, appearance (eg appearing dishevelled) or behaviour. Principle 4 also outlines that the person's past and present wishes and feelings must be taken into account (as far as possible); Blessing again could be a valuable source of support for Gordon. Principle 5 looks at carrying out the least restrictive option when restricting a person's freedom. So, it could be useful if Blessing was liaised with to see when Gordon is at his most responsive: is he better in the morning or later in the day? As Blessing is finding it difficult to cope, support may need to be provided. Various options could be considered to enable the least restrictive option; for example, would homecare support Gordon? Or if considering residential care, would a care home be less restrictive than a psychiatric unit?

A person's capacity is tested by using a two-stage test (s2, s3). So, returning to the case study of Gordon, it needs to be firstly established whether Gordon has permanent impairment (s2). It could be argued he does because of his condition, Alzheimer's disease, which affects his memory, thinking and behaviour. Secondly, can Gordon retain information, understand information relevant to a decision or weigh up information as part of the process of making the decision (s3)? If he cannot, then Gordon would be assessed as lacking capacity.

If the time came when Gordon would need to be deprived of his liberty to safeguard and protect him, Liberty Protection Safeguards (LPS), which arose as a result of the 2019 amendments to the Mental Capacity Act 2005, may be in Gordon's best interests.

When considering best interests (s4), it is essential to consider difference and diversity, for example beliefs and cultural values (s1, Principle 4). So, when considering what would be in Gordon's best interests, his wishes and feelings would be ascertained (as far as is possible), liaising with Blessing as she is the person that knows him best. A best interests meeting would enable the social worker to liaise with people that can inform decisions made for Gordon and in his best interests. So, to summarise any decisions made must be in the person's best interests (s1, Principle 1, s4).

REFERENCES

Evans, M and Harvey, D (2022) *Social Work Law: Using the Law in Practice*. St Albans: Critical Publishing.

Great Britain. Mental Capacity Act 2005. London: HMSO.

Great Britain. Mental Capacity (Amendment) Act 2019. London: HMSO.

Our note to you

○ Consider 'our note to you' as discussed previously; the same advice would apply for the Mental Capacity Act 2005 responses.

Case study 3: Pierre, a 40 year-old man (refer to the case study as outlined earlier for full details)

Question: Explain how the Care Act 2014 might apply in this case study, including how Pierre's needs for care and support could meet the eligibility criteria threshold.

Possible response

The Care Act 2014 outlines that there is a need to assess any individual who appears to need care and support, whether the individual is likely to be eligible for state-funded care or not (Evans and Harvey, 2022). Although the local authority has a duty to promote Pierre's well-being (s1) and to meet his needs for care and support (s18), Pierre would need to be assessed (s9) to see if he fulfils the eligibility criteria (s13). There are certain conditions that must be met to meet the eligibility criteria, and these include: 1) that the individual's needs for care and support arise from or are related to a physical or mental impairment or illness and are not caused by other circumstantial factors. 2) As a result of the individual's needs, the person is unable to achieve two or more of the outcomes specified in the regulations, for example, caring for nutritional needs, toilet needs, personal hygiene, wearing appropriate clothing, maintaining a liveable home environment, etc. 3) As a result of being unable to achieve these outcomes, there is, or there is likely to be, a significant effect on the individual's well-being. As Pierre's toilet needs have altered due to the accident and his personal hygiene has deteriorated due to depression, he is unable to meet two outcomes and would meet the eligibility criteria (s13).

Although there are five parts to the Act (Care and Support, Care Standards, Health, Health and Social Care, and General), Part 1 Care and Support would provide Pierre with the support he would need, especially eligibility for support under section 77 due to its requirement to provide adult social care services to adults with disabilities (Evans and Harvey, 2022). Other aspects to consider when supporting Pierre would be the requirement for an assessment of financial resources (s17) and possible provision of direct payments (s33), while at all times promoting diversity and equality in provision of services (s6).

The case study highlights that Pierre's wife Xia has decided that she cannot care for Pierre. If the situation had been different and she had offered care and support a carer's assessment (s10) could have been conducted. Pierre is presenting as self-neglecting; therefore, he may need to be safeguarded (s42–s47).

→

Even though Pierre has an impairment/disability, he will need to give consent; if he did not consent, perhaps information and advice could be provided (s4). If Pierre does consent, sections 24 to 30 outline next steps after assessment, for example, the importance of care and support plans (s25) and reviewing the care and support plan (s27).

REFERENCES

Great Britain. Care Act 2014. London: HMSO.

Evans, M and Harvey, D (2022) *Social Work Law: Using the Law in Practice*. St Albans: Critical Publishing.

Our note to you

○   Again consider 'our note to you' as discussed previously.

○   Remember the Care Act 2014 is vast; be selective in your choice of application to practice. Ensure you read the question correctly to provide the best possible responses and integration of the case study.

Case study 4: Aayansh, a 23 year-old man (refer to the case study as outlined earlier for full details)

Question: Explain the role of the Approved Mental Health Professional (AMHP) and then explain how you would use the Mental Health Act 1983/2007 in practice to support and safeguard Aayansh.

Possible response

Approved Mental Health Professionals (AMHP) are mental health professionals who work in conjunction with medical professionals and have been approved by a local social services authority to carry out certain duties under the Mental Health Act 2007 amendments of the 1983 Mental Health Act. They are responsible for co-ordinating the assessment under the Mental Health Act (MHA) 1983 (s2, first section, s3, sectioned previously) for a person experiencing mental health problems and admission to hospital if the person is sectioned. The AMHP role includes interviewing in a suitable manner, making the application for detention (MHA 1983, s13), arranging for transport for the person to be taken to hospital, ensuring that pets are placed and property is secure, completing a report of the assessment for the receiving hospital/ward containing future recommendations in relation to aftercare and supervision/management, applying to the Justice of the Peace for a warrant to search for and remove patients (MHA 1983, s135), making an application to County Court to displace or appoint a nearest relative (MHA 1983, s26); the nearest relative (NR) can be nominated by the patient's wife or husband, eldest child, parent, sibling or grandchildren or grandparent. The AMHP may also be involved (MHA 1983, s117) in discharge planning if the person has been sectioned previously.

Although other professionals such as an occupational therapist and chartered psychologist can be the AMHP, Greta is the social worker, and an AMHP, so can co-ordinate Aayansh's assessment. As Aayansh has attempted to jump from his flat on the third floor, is presenting mental health issues in a public place and is considered to need immediate care and control, the police have holding powers under the MHA 1983 (s136), which enables Aayansh to be taken to a place of safety where he can be assessed by a doctor and then an AMHP. Greta would need to liaise with Aayansh's mum and GP to access medical files to see if there is a previous history of mental health problems since the section of the Mental Health Act under which the application is made will depend on whether it is the first time (s2) Aayansh has been subject to sectioning or if he has previous history (s3). Aayansh could be subject to 72 hours' compulsory admission (s4) or be prevented from discharge from hospital (s5) because Aayansh's mother Amayra said that Aayansh has been expressing bizarre beliefs over the past three weeks; for example, he has stated that his mother has been replaced by a robot and he has also stopped eating because he claims that there are people in his food. Although it does not apply to Aayansh, as he is unable to give consent, s131 relates to informal consent if a person has capacity and can consent, while s37 outlines that a person with mental health issues can go to hospital instead of prison.

REFERENCES

Evans, M and Harvey, D (2022) *Social Work Law: Using the Law in Practice*. St Albans: Critical Publishing.

Great Britain. Mental Health Act 1983/2007. London: HMSO.

Our note to you

○ Again, refer to the note guidance for the Children Act 1989/2004, Mental Capacity Act 2005 and Care Act 2014.

○ As with the Children Act 1989/2004, if you refer to an amendment to the Act, ensure the reader knows to which part of the Act you are referring; make it clear. So, if you are referring to the Mental Health Act 1983 make it clear and if you are referring to the 2007 amendment make it clear.

Points to remember

- In the exam read the question carefully.

- Ensure you refer to the legislation you are being asked to consider; if you discuss legislation other that what you are being asked to consider you will lose marks.

- Allocate your time wisely; decide how long you will allocate to each question and stick to it. Otherwise you may find you do not have enough time to answer one of the questions and may lose marks.

- Allow some time to read through your work. Check grammar, spelling and presentation; although allowance may be made for exam nerves on the day, you want to be proud of your submission.

- Once you have submitted your exam paper, forget about it; there is nothing you can do until you get the result.

ESSAY PREPARATION

As with exam preparation, refer to the mindmaps you have been using; remember which colour refers to which Act of Parliament to prompt you. Refer back to the key points indicated in each chapter and reflect upon your personal reflections and individual thoughts. The difference between exams and essays is that to a degree when you undertake an exam, nerves are taken into account and expectations regarding presentation and reference provision are not as high. Therefore, when writing an essay, key points need to be taken into account, which will be explored next.

Key points to remember when writing essays

- Present your essay well from the outset; it helps to form the marker's first impression of your essay; for example, be consistent with font size and style, usually Arial 12 pt and double spaced, which also makes it easier for the marker to read.

- Provide a clear introduction, outline what you will be considering in the essay and then ensure you cover all those points.

- Ensure that in the body of the essay, you cover all the points. You might wish to write them down and tick them off or cross them out as you cover them.

- Be a critical thinker; look for comparisons, strengths and limitations.

- Provide a strong conclusion. Summarise what you have been considering in the essay and do not provide any new information; the conclusion is a summary.

Referencing tips

- Provide a page number if making a direct quote, for example '*social workers need to be guided by the law*' (Green, 2021, p 1); if it is by two authors use (Green and Green, 2021, p 1); if it is by more than two, you name the first author then use et al, eg (Green et al, 2021, p 1).

- If you are summarising the author's information, you only provide the author's surname(s) and year, not a page number, so for example: the law guides social workers (Green, 2021); again, if it is by two authors (Green and Green, 2021) and if it is by more than two (Green et al, 2021).

- Authors' initials do not go in the body of the assignment but are required in the reference list (see essay example reference list).

- Ensure you read widely and provide these references throughout your essay, ensuring you reference right at the start of your essay. If you see large chunks of text with no references, go back and re-read and change if necessary to see which references you can include. Wider reading not only informs your academic thinking but also can impact the quality of your writing. Wider reading includes books, journal articles, reports, and so on, not just internet sites.

- Ensure the reference list only has the references you have used in the essay and they are correct in format and are in alphabetical order.

- Check which referencing style is required by your institution. It could be Harvard or another style; consult the library for support.

Shortened version of what an essay could look like

Possible essay response

In this essay the Care Act 1989 and the 2004 amendment will be applied to the case study of Sarah and Tim. Sarah and Tim are under 18 years of age and would be supported by the Children Act 1989/2004 (Evans and Harvey, 2022). The Children Act section 1 outlines that the welfare of the child is paramount (Johns, 2017; Diaz, 2020) and as such the local authority has a duty of care towards the children following Miss Okuntunde's referral to social services.

Section 17 of the Children Act 1989 would classify the children as children in need because they have mild–moderate learning disabilities (Adams and Leshone, 2016; O'Loughlin and O'Loughlin, 2016). An amendment of the Children Act in 2004 placed duties on the local authority to support children up to a maximum

$\longrightarrow$

age of 25 years if the children were to become looked after by the local authority before they were 16 years old (Children Act 2004, s9). Therefore, if Sarah and Tim were to become looked after before the age of 16, they could receive child-centred local authority support up to the age of 25 years. Under the 2004 amendment of the Children Act 1989, Sarah's and Tim's wishes and feelings (s53) would need to be considered as well as the impact their home life may have on their educational achievement (s52).

As Sarah has bruising on her legs, this could indicate a risk of physical abuse and provides reasonable cause to suspect that Sarah and Tim are suffering, or are likely to suffer, significant harm (Children Act 1989, s47), which places a duty on the local authority to investigate (Gov.UK, 2015; Gov.UK, 2018). Such an investigation would require allocating a social worker to the case to conduct an assessment (Ferguson, 2017; Evans and Harvey, 2022).

The social worker would need to speak to Sarah and Tim at school and also conduct a home visit (Ferguson, 2017). On the way to the visit, the social worker may be considering various options depending on the situation; for example, if Sarah and Tim were at risk of significant harm (s47) and needed to be accommodated, it would be better if Sarah and Tim's parents agreed to voluntary accommodation (s20) as this would lessen anxiety for the children (Evans and Harvey, 2022). However, if Sarah and Tim were at risk of significant harm (s47) and their parents did not engage, in order for the children to be safeguarded the children may be accommodated under an interim care order (s38) or full care order (s31) contingent on the individual situation.

If the situation worsened, the parents were not engaging and Sarah and Tim were considered to be at immediate risk of significant harm (s47), an emergency protection order (EPO, s44) may be applied for; this may also require support from the police (s46; Cocker and Allain, 2011).

Unwin and Hogg (2012) discuss effective social work with children and families and give guidance on how to practise effectively. So, if after conducting an assessment and effective social work practice Sarah and Tim's parents do engage because they recognise they need help with the children's behaviour and the way they deal with it, Sarah, Tim and their parents may be supported under the Children Act 1989 (s17). As the '*the basic premise is that children's well-being is best promoted by encouraging and supporting them to live with their own families, and everything should be done to facilitate this*' (Johns, 2017, p 61), if Sarah and Tim can remain at home this would be the best outcome. However, if at any time they are at risk of significant harm all efforts should be made to safeguard them (Evans and Harvey, 2022).

REFERENCES

Adams, J and Leshone, D (2016) *Active Social Work with Children with Disabilities*. St Albans: Critical Publishing.

Children Act 1989 [online] Available at: www.legislation.gov.uk/ukpga/1989/41/contents (accessed 4 March 2022).

Children Act 2004 [online] Available at: www.legislation.gov.uk/ukpga/2004/31 (accessed 4 March 2022).

Cocker, C and Allain, L (2011) *Advanced Social Work with Children and Families*. London: Learning Matters Ltd.

Diaz, C (2020) *Decision Making in Child and Family Social Work*. Bristol: Policy Press.

Evans, M and Harvey, D (2022) *Social Work Law: Using the Law in Practice*. St Albans: Critical Publishing.

Ferguson, H (2017) How Children Become Invisible in Child Protection Work: Findings from Research into Day-to-Day Social Work Practice. *British Journal of Social Work*, 47: 1007–23.

Gov.UK (2015) *What to Do if You Are Worried a Child is Being Abused*. [online] Available at: https://assets.publishing.service.gov.uk/government/uploads/system/uploads/attachment_data/file/419604/What_to_do_if_you_re_worried_a_child_is_being_abused.pdf (accessed 4 March 2022).

Gov.UK (2018) *Working Together to Safeguard Children*. [online] Available at: www.gov.uk/government/publications/working-together-to-safeguard-children–2 (accessed 4 March 2022).

Johns, R (2017) *Using the Law in Social Work*. London: Sage.

O'Loughlin, M and O'Loughlin, S (2016) *Social Work with Children and Families*. London: Sage/Learning Matters Ltd.

Unwin, P and Hogg, R (2012) *Effective Social Work with Children and Families*. London: Sage.

Although we have considered just one of the four case studies, the key points to remember would apply when writing any law essay.

APPLYING THE LAW ON PLACEMENT

On placement, the Professional Capabilities Framework (PCF) needs to be fulfilled. This is a framework for practice and learning to define your capabilities, progress your social work career and develop your practice knowledge and skills for nine levels of social work in England (BASW, 2021a); these include: professionalism, values and ethics, diversity and equality, rights, justice and economic well-being, knowledge, critical reflection and analysis, skills and interventions, contexts and organisations, and professional leadership.

The PCF supports social workers to meet the regulatory requirements for social work practice and is aligned with the International Federation of Social Workers (IFSW, 2021), the global body for the social work profession, to enable a consistent approach to social work practice. The fifth domain relates to knowledge, which includes developing and applying knowledge in relation to social work law, thus highlighting the importance of understanding and applying social work law since without passing all nine domains you will be unable to practise as a social worker.

> Critically reflect upon which laws would be used on your placement. Then think about how this impacts your practice. Did the law work effectively in practice and did it support the persons with whom you worked?

POST QUALIFYING

The PCF also works in conjunction with the Knowledge and Skills Statements (KSS) (2015a), which are post-qualifying standards social workers need to meet in their Assessed and Supported Year in Employment (ASYE) (DfE, 2019; BASW, 2021b). The ASYE also gives newly qualified social workers extra support during their first year of employment when working with vulnerable children, families and adults (DfE, 2015a, 2015b). Thus, utilising PCF frameworks (BASW, 2021a) and the policy and practice guidance of the KSS (DfE, 2015a) can work together for best practice. So, considering the array of constraints within which you will be working and the accountabilities you will be responsible for, understanding and applying the law is essential.

CHAPTER SUMMARY

The intention in this chapter was to prepare you for applying law to practice when undertaking a law exam or law essay, on placement and in early practice. As outlined, institutional guidance will vary and you need to ensure you follow your own institution guidelines, using the material in this chapter for guidance only. We have only one more thing to say: we wish you well in your exams, essays and placements and, when qualified, be proud of your achievements.

REFERENCES

British Association of Social Workers (BASW) (2021a) Professional Capabilities Framework. [online] Available at: www.basw.co.uk/professional-development/professional-capabilities-framework-pcf (accessed 4 March 2022).

British Association of Social Workers (BASW) (2021b) PCF – End of Last Placement/Completion. [online] Available at: www.basw.co.uk/professional-development/professional-capabilities-framework-pcf/the-pcf/last-placement (accessed 4 March 2022).

Department for Education (DfE) (2015a) Social Work Post-qualifying Standards: Knowledge and Skills Statements/Supporting Vulnerable Children and Their Families. [online] Available at: www.gov.uk/government/publications/knowledge-and-skills-statements-for-child-and-family-social-work (accessed 4 March 2022).

Department for Education (DfE) (2015b) Adult Social Work: Knowledge. [online] Available at: www.gov.uk/government/consultations/adult-social-work-knowledge-and-skills (accessed 4 March 2022).

Department for Education (DfE) (2019) Assessed and Supported Year in Employment. [online] Available at: www.gov.uk/government/publications/assessed-and-supported-year-in-employment-asye/assessed-and-supported-year-in-employment (accessed 4 March 2022).

International Federation of Social Workers (2021) Information Hub. [online] Available at: www.ifsw.org (accessed 4 March 2022).

Mental Capacity Act 2005 [online] Available at: www.legislation.gov.uk/ukpga/2005/9/contents (accessed 4 March 2022).

CONCLUSION

12 Conclusion

INTRODUCTION

This chapter briefly summarises the preceding chapters, taking you on a legislative journey from the first chapter to the last in a concise and easy-to-read manner, all the while considering why we focused on each chapter, and why it was important to social work practice, together with key points relevant to each chapter.

CHAPTER SUMMARIES

Chapter 1

Chapter 1 introduces the book and outlines techniques used throughout the book to make the law more accessible, such as mindmaps, case studies and key points to remember. There are also tasks to test your legislative knowledge, and opportunities to consider anti-discriminatory or anti-oppressive practice issues, as well as activities to capture personal reflection and individual thoughts.

Chapter 2

Chapter 2 introduces the English legal system and social work. The English legal system is a significant aspect of private and public law proceedings; criminal proceedings (Children Act 1989, s21); children becoming looked after (Children Act 1989, s20, s31, s38); children being safeguarded (Children Act 1989, s47), mental health (Children Act 1989, s25), mental capacity and best interests hearings. This chapter is important to social work practice because you need to understand the roles of the different professionals involved in court proceedings and implications for social work practice.

Key points relevant to this chapter

Remember that social work as a profession does not require you to be legally trained. The PCFs consider knowledge of the law, so the process you should engage in is becoming conversant with aspects of the law that deal directly with your practice. Also highlighted in this chapter was that the English legal system is made up of legislation that relates to England and Wales and that different courts have specific roles and powers within legislation.

Chapter 3

This chapter is the first of three that focus on child legislation and begins with children in need or at risk of significant harm (Children Act 1989, s47). It is important to social work practice because often when the words child protection, child safeguarding or risk of significant harm arise, professional anxiety can be experienced. However, this chapter shows that as long as you work within the constraints of the law, work in partnership with other agencies and gain a sound understanding of how to apply law to practice, you will feel better able to practise effectively within this field of social work practice.

Key points relevant to this chapter

- You must establish if a child is at risk of harm. While this particular aspect of social work requires you to be able to make quick and effective decisions, you must always take a minute and think about your decision before rushing in.

- If there are concerns about significant harm then a strategy meeting must take place, and a decision on how best to safeguard the child/children must be made. Action must be taken in a timely manner to avoid delays.

- Remember the local authority has a legal team who are available to give you advice. If in doubt, consult your legal team, line manager or senior manager.

Chapter 4

This chapter focuses on child legislation and explores what happens when children become looked after and the process of a child being accommodated or cared for in alternative arrangements. This chapter will enable you to understand the procedures embedded within specific childcare legislation that allow the state to intervene and place children and young people into a regulated placement either voluntarily (Children Act 1989, s20), under an interim care order (Children Act 1989, s38) or under a care order (Children Act 1989, s31). It is important to social work practice because social workers need to understand the intricacies of child-focused law to ensure the welfare of the children and young people is paramount (Children Act 1989, s1)

Key points relevant to this chapter

- Legal routes for children to become looked after include: voluntary, where a parent agrees that the local authority will look after their child for a short period of time to cover a family crisis (Children Act 1989, s20) or statutory, where the court decides that a child should be remanded as a result of committing a serious offence (Children Act 1989, s21) or if a child is at risk of significant harm (Children Act 1989, s47).

- The local authority as far as possible should try to keep the child within the family home with support. Where this is not possible, a plan should be made that involves extended family members to maintain that child's connections, identity and cultural needs.

- If the local authority is considering a placement outside of the extended family network, then a permanency plan (assessing and preparing the child/ young person for long-term care) must be considered.

Chapter 5

Chapter 5 considers children in the criminal justice system and provides background on the processes of working with children and young people who behave anti-socially or commit offences. It is important because social workers need to understand how to apply legislation pertaining to the criminal justice system (Crime and Disorder Act 1998, Part 1) in practice, depending whether it is the child/young person's first offence or whether the offence is serious.

Key points relevant to this chapter

- If it is the child/young person's first offence, the options available to them will be different than if they have previous convictions, depending on what those previous convictions are.

- Children and young people who get into trouble for the first time or for less serious offences can be dealt with informally by the police. If a child is interviewed and admits to doing something wrong, the police could consider out-of-court disposals, for example triage, which is recorded on the police national computer as no further action, community resolution or youth cautions.

Chapter 6

This chapter discusses the Mental Capacity Act (MCA) 2005 in the context of how it applies to practice with adults and when a child is transitioning from child to adult services. The MCA applies to all people over the age of 16 years who live in England and Wales and who may lack the capacity to make all or some decisions for themselves. It provides the legal framework to assess if an individual can make decisions for themselves or, if they lack the capacity, to facilitate a plan of action to act in the person's best interests (s4). It is important to social work practice because social workers need to understand how to support vulnerable adults to be empowered within their personal circumstances and to contribute to decision making which acts in the best interests (s4, s1, Principle 4) of the people with whom you are working.

Key points relevant to this chapter

- Remember that everyone is an individual when applying the law. Two people may have Alzheimer's disease but their condition will be unique to them; thus, applying legislation needs to be tailored to the individual and it is not a case of one size fits all.

- While a person may be deemed to lack capacity (s2, s3) on some issues, they may have capacity to make other decisions such as what to eat or wear.

- The law is a tool to support and protect the people with whom you work and should be applied appropriately.

Chapter 7

Chapter 7 explores Deprivation of Liberty Safeguards (DoLS) and Liberty Protection Safeguards (LPS) in the context of application to social work practice. We focused on this because life is unpredictable and an individual never knows when they may be in a position where they are in need of being safeguarded by depriving them of their liberty. This is important to social work practice because social work support may be needed in safeguarding situations and social workers need to understand how to practise in harmony with not only DoLS and LPS but also other legislation such as the Mental Capacity Act 2005 (Chapter 6) and the Care Act 2014 (Chapter 10) to ensure best practice in the best interests of the person with whom they are working in partnership.

Key points relevant to this chapter

Remember that DoLS and LPS are frameworks to ensure best interests, protection and safeguarding of individuals if they are deemed to lack capacity, and are essential to contribute to good social work practice. As we learned from Bournewood Hospital and Winterbourne View, even though frameworks are put into place to protect vulnerable people who lack capacity, these can be susceptible to abuse. As a social worker you need to understand DoLS and LPS and how to apply them in practice to safeguard and protect the people with whom you are working.

Chapter 8

This chapter considers the Mental Health Act 1983 and the 2007 amendment to the Act. As highlighted in this chapter, the main purpose of the Mental Health Act 1983/2007 is to assess, treat and uphold the rights of people who experience mental health issues when they are at risk of harm to themselves or other people and may be sectioned (s2, s3). We focused on this chapter because social workers need to understand mental health legislation to support people experiencing mental health problems. This chapter is important to social work practice because, as Marshal et al (2020) highlight, during the Covid-19 pandemic, concern for people's mental health has risen, due to individuals worrying about the effect Covid-19 will have on their lives and worrying about their future; these changes have the potential to increase the need for social work support.

Key points relevant to this chapter

Remember that although the Mental Health Act 1983 and the 2007 amendment are complex areas of legislation, you do not need to memorise every single section, but just to have a sound foundation knowledge of it. The important point is to understand how to access information when you need it, for example by looking at government guidelines and specialist organisations and working with other professionals and experts by experience who have greater knowledge and wider experience.

Chapter 9

This chapter discusses legislation pertaining to disability/impairment seen and unseen. We focused on this because not all disability is visible; for example, if a person is using a wheelchair, the disability may be evident but if a person experiences sight or hearing impairment and does not use visual aids to denote impairment(s), then the impairment may be unseen. This chapter is important to social work practice because when social workers work with people with impairments/disabilities, disability diversity and each individual's need must be addressed so that individualised support can be provided. Understanding and applying legislation effectively contributes to this.

Key points relevant to this chapter

Legislation pertaining to disability both seen and unseen can appear complex as you may need to refer to various legislation for guidance. A useful point of contact can be specialist organisations, for example Sense, who work with people who experience D/deafblindness, or the NDCS, who work with children who experience Deafness and their families/carers.

Chapter 10

This chapter discusses the Care Act 2014, adult care and support. We focused on this in this chapter to encourage you to acquire legislative knowledge to enable you to assess the needs of (s9), consider the diversity of (s6) and provide the best service to vulnerable adults and their carers (s10) if they meet the eligibility criteria (s13). This chapter highlights that the main area of the Act you will need to understand in practice is Part 1, Care and Support, as well as the six key principles to safeguarding. This chapter is important to social work practice because the Care Act 2014 outlines the need to assess any individual who appears to need care and support, whether the individual is likely to be eligible for state-funded care or not, and you will need to understand how to apply this legislation in practice if you are working with adults.

Key points relevant to this chapter

The Care Act 2014's framework indicates that there is a need to assess individuals who present as needing care and support, whether the individual is likely to be eligible for state-funded care or not. However, it is important to remember that consent is required from an individual before they are assessed. As with other legislation, if as a social worker you are not familiar with the Care Act 2014 you will not be able to apply it in practice.

Chapter 11

This chapter focuses on building your study skills in relation to essays, exams and placements. We focused on this because we can teach you the law and broaden your legislative knowledge but you also need confidence to apply knowledge of the law in practice. To enable you to have a clearer understanding of how to improve your study skills, four Acts were focused upon, the Children Act 1989/2004, Care Act 2014, Mental Capacity Act 2005/2019 and Mental Health Act 1983/2007. In this chapter you were encouraged to reflect upon the case studies, decisions made in the case studies, key points to remember, test your legislative knowledge and personal reflective activities as well as use mindmaps. This is important to social work practice because you need to understand how to successfully pass the academic and practical requirements for a social work degree to practise as a social worker. As a social worker you will be required to represent, support, empower and advocate for some of the most vulnerable people in society and as such you need to be able to articulate messages you want to convey to effectively support the people with whom you are working.

Key points relevant to this chapter

- Being committed and dedicated to your social work studies and working hard to apply the law in your law exams and essays and while out on placement will enable you to practise more effectively when qualified and practising as a social worker.

- Application of legislation to practice is essential to enable you to work in the best interests of the people with whom you are working.

- Remember, you will not know everything just because you now hold a degree qualification; education is life-long.

- Post qualifying you will need to be registered and advise the regulatory body, currently Social Work England, of any changes which may affect your ability to practise as a social worker.

- Learn from others, for example, experts by experience and professionals with more experience.

- You do not have to memorise every aspect of the law but ensure you have a good foundation and undertake further research when you need more in-depth knowledge to support the people with whom you are working.

NOTE TO YOU, FROM US, THE AUTHORS

We hope you have enjoyed using this book in your studies or early practice to enhance your understanding of how the law is applied in practice and the law's significance in decision making. A key feature is that social workers have to be mindful that social work is a people profession, where social workers manage risk and use the law when needed in the best interests of the person they are working in partnership with; it is person appropriate. As highlighted, the law is important because when making decisions the law is relevant to practice. Our initial intention was to make learning and applying the law achievable and remove the daunting feelings some of you may feel when first embarking on your law module within your social work degree programme. However, the intention is also for the book to be useful for you when you become a newly qualified social worker in practice. As highlighted, this book could additionally be beneficial for practice educators or on-site supervisors supporting their students on placement or lecturers using the book to support their teaching by using case studies, mindmaps, key points to remember, test your legislative knowledge and activities to capture personal reflection and individual thoughts.

Finally, we wish you, our readers, all the best as you begin your social work career, and in the future as you continue your professional development.

Kind regards
Michelle and Denise

REFERENCES

Marshal, L, Bibby, J and Abbs, I (2020) Emerging Evidence on COVID-19's Impact on Mental Health and Health Inequalities. The Health Foundation. Available at: www.health.org.uk/news-and-comment/blogs/emerging-evidence-on-covid-19s-impact-on-mental-health-and-health (accessed 4 March 2022).

Answers to test questions

CHAPTER 2 ANSWERS

Name five people can you expect to see if you attend court.

- barristers (prosecution and defence);
- solicitors and legal executives;
- magistrates (lay and stipendiary magistrates);
- court clerk;
- ushers;
- jurors;
- judges (different levels);
- police officers;
- social workers – *you*;
- probation and youth offending officers;
- guardians;
- expert witnesses – this could also be *you*;
- security and prison officers.

What are the three main characteristics that make laws different from simple rules?

- Laws are set and established and enforced by government.
- Laws are mandatory.
- Laws involve consequences, which are enforced through the legal system (in the UK this is usually the courts though it can be tribunals).

What seven things constitute the English legal system?

- law-making bodies, eg parliament, judiciary, legislature;
- those that enforce the law;
- institutions, processes and personnel that contribute to the operation and enforcement of the law;
- workings of the courts and tribunals;
- legal professionals;
- police, prosecutors, jurors;

- organisations that support access to justice, eg Citizen Advice Bureau, legal aid, law shops, advocacy projects.

What are the three main criminal courts in England and Wales?

- Crown Court;

- Youth Court;

- Magistrates' Court.

Name three courts a social worker might attend.

- Youth Court for criminal matters;

- Family Court;

- Court of Protection.

What is the difference between a duty and a power?

Duty: If there is a duty placed on a local authority or social worker then, whatever that duty is, it has to be carried out.

Power: If a local authority or social worker is provided with the power to undertake an act, then there is no obligation to carry out that act.

Name one difference between private law and public law.

Private law deals with a dispute between individuals and public law involves the state.

Name at least four types of courts and explain what they do.

- Supreme Court;

- Court of Appeal;

- High Court;

- Crown Court;

- Magistrates Court;

- Youth Court;

- Family Court;

- County Court.

CHAPTER 3 ANSWERS

Is the promotion of 'well-being' a duty or a power?

It is a duty, as outlined in section 1 of the Children Act 1989.

Outline three things the court considers as part of the welfare checklist.

- the wishes and feelings of the child (ensuring that these are ascertained in an age-appropriate way);

- physical, emotional and educational needs;
- the impact of any change of circumstances on the child;
- a child's age, gender, background, and any other characteristic that can be considered of importance;
- any harm which the child has suffered or is at risk of suffering;
- the parent's ability to meet the needs of the child.

Is significant harm defined in law? What issues do you think this raises for local authorities?

No – this raises issues around difference in practice from each local authority.

What three factors are considered in an assessment of children in need?

- child development;
- parenting capacity;
- family and environmental factors.

Which section of the Children Act 1989 provides a definition of 'children in need'?

Section 17.

Name two agencies that may be involved in a section 47 enquiry.

- police;
- education;
- health.

What is an EPO and when can this be applied for?

Emergency protection order – this can be applied for when there are concerns of significant harm and the child needs to be removed in an emergency.

When is a PPO used?

In cases where it has not been possible to apply for an EPO and the child will be at risk of significant harm.

CHAPTER 4 ANSWERS

List three parental risk factors that may lead to a child becoming looked after.

Any three of the following are acceptable answers:

- substance misuse;
- death;
- parental mental health;
- physical health issues;
- domestic abuse;

- ○ imprisonment;
- ○ parental learning disability;
- ○ disability.

What are the legal routes to children becoming looked after?

- ○ Section 20 accommodation – where a parent asks the local authority to accommodate their child while they maintain their parental responsibility.
- ○ Section 21 – where a child is in police detention or remand.
- ○ Where a child has offended, and it is serious enough to warrant the court deciding that they should be looked after by children's social care rather than at home until the court process is concluded.
- ○ Sections 38 and 31 – where an interim order or care order allows the local authority to share parental responsibility to make decisions about the long-term care of a child.

Name two orders that allow the local authority to plan for the long-term care of a child (these give them parental responsibility).

- ○ Section 31 Interim Care Order;
- ○ Section 38 Care Order.

Name three key pieces of legislation and how they relate to looked after children.

Any one of these legislation:

- ○ Children Act 1989;
- ○ The Children Act 1989 guidance and regulations. Volume 2: Care planning, placement and case review;
- ○ Care Standards Act 2000;
- ○ Adoption and Social Work Act 2002;
- ○ Children Act 2004;
- ○ Children and Young Person's Act 2008;
- ○ Children and Families Act 2014;
- ○ Children and Social Work Act 2017.

What is family and friends care?

Where a child is cared for by extended family or family friends; this is often referred to as Reg 24 care or connected persons.

What is an advantage of long-term fostering?

- ○ promotes permanency;
- ○ gives child a sense of belonging.

Name at least one local authority duty to looked after children.

Any one of the following is a suitable answer.

○ Section 22(3) of the Children Act 1989 sets out the general duty of the local authority looking after a child to safeguard and promote the welfare of the child. This duty underpins all activity by the local authority in relation to looked after children. This duty has become known as 'corporate parenting'. In simple terms, 'corporate parenting' means the collective responsibility of the council, elected members, employees and partner agencies for providing the best possible care and safeguarding for the children who are looked after by the council.

○ Section 22A imposes a duty on the responsible authority when a child is in their care to provide the child with accommodation.

○ Section 22B sets out the duty of the responsible authority to maintain a looked after child in other respects apart from providing accommodation.

○ Section 22C sets out the ways in which the looked after child is to be accommodated.

○ Section 22D imposes a duty on the responsible authority to formally review the child's case before making alternative arrangements for accommodation.

What are the advantages of adoption?

○ Adopters gain parental responsibility.

○ Gives a child a sense of belonging.

CHAPTER 5 ANSWERS

Name three pieces of legislation that relate to young people who offend.

Any three of the following are acceptable answers:

○ Crime and Disorder Act 1998;

○ Police and Criminal Evidence Act (PACE) 1984;

○ Criminal Justice and Immigration Act 2008;

○ Legal Aid Sentencing and Punishment of Offenders 2012;

○ Children Act 1989;

○ Criminal Justice Act 2003.

What is the principal aim of the youth justice system?

○ It shall be the principal aim of the youth justice system to prevent offending by children and young persons.

○ In addition to any other duty to which they are subject, it shall be the duty of all persons and bodies carrying out functions in relation to the youth justice system to have regard to that aim.

Which Act brought about the formation of the Youth Justice Board and the youth offending teams?

Crime and Disorder Act 1998.

At what age is a child criminally responsible in England and Wales?

Ten years-old.

Which 2008 Act brought about a reform of sentences for young people?

Criminal Justice and Immigration Act 2008.

What is the name of the community order that was introduced for youth in 2008?

Youth rehabilitation order (YRO).

Name three requirements that could be added to a youth rehabilitation order.

Any three of the following are acceptable answers:

o   attendance centre;

o   activity requirement;

o   drug testing;

o   drug treatment;

o   education;

o   electronic monitoring;

o   exclusion;

o   curfew;

o   intoxicating substance treatment;

o   local authority residence;

o   mental health treatment programme;

o   prohibited activity;

o   residence requirement;

o   supervision;

o   unpaid work;

o   intensive fostering;

o   intensive supervision and surveillance.

Which two Acts refer to appropriate adults?

Police and Criminal Evidence Act 1984 and Crime and Disorder Act 1998.

What is a specified offence? (Schedule 15 offence)

A specified offence is a violent, sexual or terrorism offence listed in Schedule 15 of the Criminal Justice Act 2003.

CHAPTER 6 ANSWERS

How many parts are there to the Mental Capacity Act 2005 and what are they?

There are three parts to the Act: Part 1 covers persons who lack capacity (s1–s62), Part 2 covers the Court of Protection and the Public Guardian (s45–63) and Part 3 is the miscellaneous and general part (s62–s69).

What are the five principles of the Mental Capacity Act 2005? Name the section they come under.

○ Principle 1: Assume capacity unless it is established the person does not have capacity; this could be permanent lack of capacity or temporary.

○ Principle 2: A person is not to be treated as unable to make a decision unless all practicable steps have been taken without success, so everything possible must be done to try to support the person.

○ Principle 3: A person is not to be treated as unable to make a decision merely because they make an unwise decision.

○ Principle 4: Best interests cannot be determined on the grounds of age, appearance or behaviour. You must consider, so far as reasonable, the person's a) past and present wishes and feelings, b) beliefs and values that would influence decision if the person had capacity, and c) other factors the person would likely to consider if they were able to do so.

○ Principle 5: You need to check you have carried out the least restrictive option.

These five principles come under section 1 of the Mental Capacity Act 2005.

What is the two-stage test? What sections support it?

If a person's capacity is tested, it is done so by undertaking a two-stage test to determine if someone lacks capacity; sections 2 and 3 support it. First, it needs to be established whether the person has a permanent impairment (such as a brain injury) or a temporary disturbance (such as substance misuse) in the functioning of the mind or brain (s2). Second, it needs to be determined if a person is unable to make a decision (s3) for themselves if they are unable to:

○ understand information relevant to a decision;

○ retain that information;

○ use or weigh up information as part of the process of making the decision or needs.

Communication support to make the decision would need to be provided; this would include an interpreter if required (s3).

How can you ensure you practise in a service user's best interest? What sections support this?

You can ensure you practice in a service user's best interest by applying section 1, Principle 4 and section 4, and ensuring you do not determine best interest on grounds of a person's age, appearance or behaviour, as well as considering as far as possible the person's past and present wishes, feelings, beliefs and values that would influence a decision if the person did have capacity.

What is the role of the Independent Mental Capacity Advocate (IMCA) and which section support this role?

An Independent Mental Capacity Advocate (IMCA) must be appointed to anyone 16 years or over where serious medical treatment or a change of residence is proposed for a person who lacks capacity and where that person has no family or friends appropriate to consult; s35 supports this role.

What is the purpose of the Court of Protection? What section supports it?

If someone is found to lack capacity or alleged to lack capacity an application can be made to the Court of Protection under s50.

CHAPTER 7 ANSWERS

Deprivation of Liberty Safeguards

What was the result of the 2009 amendment to the MCA 2005?

The Deprivation of Liberty Safeguards (DoLs).

What age does DoLS apply?

18 years of age.

How did the case of *HL v UK 45508/99 [2004] ECHR 471I* impact the law?

DoLS was introduced following findings from the European Court of Human Rights regarding the case of *HL v UK 45508/99 [2004] ECHR 471I*, in which HL was deprived of his liberty.

Why is the Winterbourne View serious case review important?

The Winterbourne View case highlighted that human rights were not recognised and people were abused; thus safeguards such as DoLS to protect vulnerable people are essential. An application for DoLS shows that the managerial team and staff caring for vulnerable people understand that the people in their care have rights to be protected and to be treated with dignity and respect, while at all times promoting the person's best interests even if an individual is not in a position to make their own decisions.

Liberty Protection Safeguards

What was the result of the 2019 amendment?

The Liberty Protection Safeguards (LPS), which are due to come into effect in 2022.

At what age do LPS apply?

Anyone aged over 16 years.

To whom will the LPS apply when they come into effect?

LPS will apply to care homes, nursing homes, hospitals, day services, supported living, sheltered housing; they are not due to come into action until 2022.

What is the name of the replacement BIA role?

Approved Mental Capacity Professionals (AMCP).

CHAPTER 8 ANSWERS

What is section 2?

First time a person is sectioned.

What is section 3?

Where a person has been previously sectioned; after being sectioned under this section the person is entitled to support under the CPA.

What is section 26?

Nearest relative.

What does section 117 require?

Requires health and social services to provide services until those services are no longer required or the person can be transferred to the CPS.

Which two roles were introduced under the 2007 amendment of the MHA 1983?

AMHP and IMHA.

CHAPTER 9 ANSWERS

Which Act and which section gives the definition of disability?

Equality Act, section 6 provides the definition of disability, which is that a person is disabled if they have a physical or mental impairment that has a substantial long-term effect on their ability to do normal daily activities.

Which Act protects service users' and their families' human rights?

Human Rights Act 1998 – Respect service users' and their families' human rights.

Which sections of the Care Act 2014 explain how local authorities should determine who is eligible for support and provide support where appropriate?

Sections 77 and 78.

Which Act would you use to support children who experience D/deafblindness?

Local Authority and Social Services Act 1970, section 7 outlines provision with respect to the organisation, management and administration of local authority social services for children who experience D/deafblindness.

Which Act and section would you use to a) promote the welfare of a child, b) support a child with a disability and c) safeguard a child?

Children Act 1989 – a) section 1 welfare of the child is paramount, b) section 17 child in need and c) section 47 child is at risk of significant harm.

Which section of the 2004 amendment to the Children Act 1989 would you use to consider the child's wishes and feelings?

Section 53 due consideration to child's wishes and feelings.

Which Act and which part relates to children and young people with special educational needs and disabilities/impairments?

Children and Families Act 2014, Part 3, which includes sections 19–83

CHAPTER 10 ANSWERS

What is the purpose of the Care Act 2014?

The Care Act 2014 outlines that there is a need to assess any individual who appears to need care and support, whether the individual is likely to be eligible for state-funded care or not; however, consent is required from an individual before they are assessed.

How many parts are there to the Care Act 2014 and what are they?

There are five parts to the Act: Care and Support, Care Standards, Health, Health and Social Care, and General.

Which part of the Care Act 2014 would you likely use the most in your social work role?

Part 1.

Which sections of Part 1 of the Care Act 2014 would you be most likely to use in your role as a social worker?

Section 1 promoting an individual's well-being, section 4 providing information and advice, section 5 promoting diversity and quality of provision of service, section 9 assessment, section 10 carer's assessment, section 13 eligibility criteria, section 25 care plans, section 27 reviews, section 33 direct payments, sections 42 to 47 safeguarding, section 58 assessment of child's needs for adult care and support (transitioning).

What are the six key principles in safeguarding?

Empowerment, protection, prevention, proportionality, partnership and accountability.

What is an Independent Care Act Advocate (ICAA)?

An ICAA is referred by a social worker or other person to support the person to enable them to present their thoughts, feelings and views.

Index

Milton Keynes UK
Ingram Content Group UK Ltd.
UKHW051601230924
448742UK00021B/297